7 WORDS that can CHANGE YOUR LIFE

RICH POWELL

7 WORDS
that can
CHANGE
YOUR
LIFE

REALIZE *the* PURPOSE *for Which*
You Were DESIGNED

XULON ELITE

Xulon Press Elite
2301 Lucien Way #415
Maitland, FL 32751
407.339.4217
www.xulonpress.com

Paperback ISBN-13: 978-1-6628-6109-3
Hard Cover ISBN-13: 978-1-6628-6692-0
Ebook ISBN-13: 978-1-6628-6110-9

In *7 Words* Rich Powell guides the reader into a deeper understanding of the radical nature of God's gift in His Son, Jesus Christ. We are free *from* the self-destructive bonds of sin. We are free *to* live abundantly and joyously in Christ! This is solid food!

Tim Kilpatrick, M.D.

Dr. Rich Powell provides a rich resource for believers to grow in their understanding of the most foundational beliefs of Christianity in "7 Words that can Change Your Life." This work should be read by all believers who want to deepen their faith and biblical knowledge of the essential doctrines that revolve around the gospel. This work represents a deep and yet accessible study that will help every believer who reads it to strengthen their walk with Christ and live for him. This book should be read by every Christian who wants to take their faith in Jesus to the next level.

Bernard James Mauser, Director of Philosophy, Politics, & Economics, Southern Evangelical Seminary; Author, *Reading to Grow: A Field Guide to the Bible*

Dr. Rich Powell's *7 Words that can Change Your Life* addresses every person's separation from God and the simple, yet so profound only way to live fully with God: Jesus Christ. People attempt to control their own lives, but despite our hubris with science and technology that actually reveals the incredible complexity of God's creation, we retreat into ourselves. Pastor Powell outlines seven principles of God's plan for each of us to have meaningful lives, and eternal life, using biblical scriptures, the historical fact of God's gift of Christ to each of us, as well as useful observations and examples from theologians, philosophers, and scientists.

David Hollar, PhD, Associate Professor,
Mercer University School of Medicine

Be prepared for seven words that will lead you to faith or amplify your understanding of faith!

Dennis Foley, Pastor, Christian School Consultant

The author creates a perfect progression of biblical thought and scriptural evidence for how the Christian life is intentionally designed for a loving and positional relationship with the Father. Through a thoughtful study of self-preeminence, separation, and surrender, this story of relational position with Christ ends with a proclamation of our overall existence – my relationship status has been restored! My purpose has been made clear!

Wendy Barajas, Director of School Quality,
National Heritage Academy

How has our sinful condition been addressed by God? *Seven Words*, a pastor's memorable distillation of God's "good news", answers these questions with clarity and grace. Join the author in a thrilling study of God's rescue plan by unpacking the implications of these seven words for your life. I found this study immensely helpful in my own walk with Jesus.

Robert B. Swanson MD, FACS, General and
Vascular Surgeon, Roanoke, VA

Rich Powell is a pastor who throws himself fully and completely into everything that he does. This book is no exception. Rich has taken his considerable grasp of the Word and crafted something that anyone can learn from. I highly recommend it.

Allen Bacon, Clinical Mental Health Counselor
and Addiction Specialist

Great theological truths with practical applications in a readable, understandable, and logical format. Doctrinal study in a devotional style of presentation is the new methodology implied thus making this book both practical and richly research oriented. These foundational truths cannot be neglected because they cost eternity but at the same time can be challenging to understand. The author maintained the balance without diluting the truth and at the same time creating interest in the reader in the way the book was formulated.

Jacob Gaddala, Pastor, Vishakhapatnam, India

To Grace Bible Church
Winston Salem, NC.
Thank you!

Contents

Introduction

We all love good news, especially if that good news can significantly impact our lives. There are times that we hear such good news that it requires an immediate and unapologetic announcement to those around us. N.T. Wright illustrates this well:

> Imagine that you are sitting quietly in a café with a couple of friends when suddenly the door bursts open and in rushes a stranger with a wild, excited look on his face. "Good news" he shouts. "You'll never guess. The greatest news you can imagine." What on earth can he be talking about? What could his *good news* be, and why does he think it justifies barging into a café and telling strangers about it?

> Perhaps, in a region with high unemployment and poverty, he just learned that people had discovered huge new reserves of coal, oil, or gas. Suddenly there would be thousands of new jobs and a new start for everyone. I know places where that

would cause otherwise quiet people to burst into a room and shout the news to everybody. That might justify such a dramatic announcement.[1]

Regardless of your upbringing or your geography, there is one piece of news that should elicit such a response from us all – the Gospel. The gospel ("good news") of grace in Jesus Christ is simple, yet deeply profound. How can something be both simple *and* profound? *Simple* does not mean *simplistic*. The grace of Jesus Christ is free and requires only our trust, but that does not mean it was not costly. The gospel can and ought to be understood simply; but when we investigate God's work for our redemption, we just might be left in awe of the Creator and Redeemer for what he has done to accomplish it.

This book is a study to plunge into the depths of the purpose and work of God. Our objective is to deeply understand the underpinnings of the gospel. Then, in the outflow of our knowledge of God's amazing grace, we will be able to live fully in his power, and thereby point others to him.

My approach to investigate the foundations of the gospel is to mine the rich language of Scripture and uncover the value of their meaning. I will focus on seven words given to us by the Holy Spirit: Righteousness, Propitiation, Redemption, Imputation, Justification,

---

[1] N.T. Wright, *Simply Good News* (HarperCollins, 2015), pp. 1-2

Reconciliation, and Regeneration. I believe that these words are packed with significance that can be missed if not explored in light of what God has disclosed to us. There is one section in the apostle Paul's letter to the Roman church that exhibits these seven rich and meaningful truths.

After affirming his confidence in the gospel as the power of God for salvation (Romans 1:16), Paul proceeded to argue our desperate need for the gospel by demonstrating that all of humanity is under the tyranny of sin and in bondage to it by nature. Indeed, if we are honest, human depravity is the most empirically verifiable truth of the human condition. Paul, however, appealed to God's assessment of the human condition as described in the Old Testament Scriptures. The whole world is accountable to God (Romans 3:19).

Then the good news begins in Romans 3:21 with the words, "But now." It is here, and in the following three chapters, that the apostle introduced us to key truths, the seven words that communicate the amazing depths of what God has accomplished. Although these words are not used in our day-to-day conversation, these words perfectly encapsulate the message of the gospel – "the light of the knowledge of the glory of God in the face of Jesus Christ" (2 Corinthians 4:6). These are words and theological concepts that are not commonly used, but they are often staples of Christian jargon used in attempts to communicate the gospel, assuming the listener has even a clue to their meaning.

I once visited a friend in a hospital lounge who was concerned about his friend facing a life-threatening condition. He attempted to communicate the gospel to this friend, but his words were so wrapped in theological jargon that even I was having difficulty understanding. Albert Einstein is credited by many to have said, "If you can't explain it simply, you don't understand it well enough." We also must be able to explain these truths to others without leaving our hearers confused in a muddle of religious terminology. To do this, we must understand these crucial elements of the gospel and their depth for ourselves. The purpose of this study is to take these profound biblical truths – words that have rich and powerful meaning – and explain how they reveal to us the glory of God in the gospel of grace.

The meanings of these words are not hidden, nor do they require a special knowledge. These truths are embedded in Scripture as revealed to us by the Holy Spirit. Yes, there are profound depths to them – things that God does behind the scenes that require our study; but they can be understood in their simplicity. As we commit to be students of God's self-disclosure and engage it with humility, we can enjoy confidence in the clarity of Scripture. God's Spirit draws us in to his Word to delight in it. Join me in a humble, prayerful search and study into the seven words that will help us understand the wonderful works of God that can transform us.

CHAPTER 1

The Problem: **Righteousness**

Humanity cannot define nor achieve what is needed.

None is righteous, no, not one.
Romans 3:10

If only there were evil people somewhere insidiously
committing evil deeds, and it were necessary only
to separate them from the rest of us and destroy
them. But the line dividing good and evil cuts
through the heart of every human being.[2]

Alexander Solzhenitsyn

E very human heart longs for the satisfaction of a life
that is good – a life where everything is the way it
ought to be. But the realities of human injustice – abuses
of power, a senseless murder, the greedy financier, a
negligent parent, a hateful mob, a cruel colleague

---

[2] A.I. Solzhenitsyn, The Gulag Archipelago 1918-1956: An Experiment
in Literary Investigation I-II. New York, Harper & Row, 1973, page
168

– generate an unquenchable thirst for peace in the human soul. Humanity's search to build a romanticized utopia leads to competing ideals ranging from isolated autonomy to absolute control that often ends in unnecessary brutality. My naturally human idea of things being right is that I get to do, experience, and acquire what I want without restriction. But since we are designed to and must live in community, this philosophy of life simply cannot work. Living for self does not make a thriving society. If we are honest, the problem lies in every human heart, including my own. I am bent on wanting what I feel is right – for me. What you and I need is the gospel.

Living for self does not make a thriving society.

But now the righteousness of God has been manifested apart from the law, although the Law and the Prophets bear witness to it — the righteousness of God through faith in Jesus Christ for all who believe. For there is no distinction: for all have sinned and fall short of the glory of God, and are justified by his grace as a gift, through the redemption that is in Christ Jesus, whom God put forward as a propitiation by his blood, to be received by faith. This was to show God's righteousness, because in his divine forbearance he had passed over former sins. It was to show his righteousness at the present time, so that he might be just and the justifier of the one who has faith in Jesus (Romans 3:21-26).

The text above is one of the richest paragraphs in Scripture, with so much treasure to mine. Four of the words that we seek to understand in this book come directly from those six verses: *righteousness, justified, redemption*, and *propitiation*. Because we are rational and visual beings, we can *see* with our minds. Forming mental images will help us understand and remember the wealth that each of these words represents.

God's righteousness is the foundational truth, because the issue of righteousness is the core of the gospel. For humanity, the problem is that we lack righteousness and cannot attain it. Our unrighteousness exacts the required wrath of holy God (Romans 1:18) "for all his ways are justice" (Deuteronomy 32:4). Not only is God righteous – his very being defines righteousness – but also he makes righteousness available to us. We must understand this about the gospel of grace from the start. "For the LORD *is righteous;* he loves righteous deeds; the upright shall behold his face" (Psalm 11:7).

For humanity, the problem is that we lack righteousness and cannot attain it.

A Necessary Reference Point

French philosopher, Jean-Paul Sartre said, "No finite point has meaning without an infinite reference point." A reference point is something used to judge or understand something else. It is a fixed place used to help you find your way or see where other things are. For example, various studies[3] have shown that if you are walking, swimming, or driving in an open expanse, you will ultimately go in circles. You may think you are going straight, but you will just be going in circles, unless you have a reference point. When we have a fixed reference point, we can determine where we are going. A compass is also the perfect example of this. Although a compass has arrows to show us where we are going, it is only useful if we know that it has a fixed reference point. For a compass to be useful and trustworthy, it must have a fixed reference point so you know your direction and progress.

Righteousness can be understood as *the way life should be*, or the way *I* should be. The Greek word Paul used for *righteousness* means to put right with, or to cause to be in a right relationship with, so the concept of righteousness assumes a standard. Everyone has a differing opinion about how life should be, or about how you or I should be. So which one of us is right? This presents a crucial dilemma in the human experience.

---

[3] For example, a video featured on NPR, https://www.youtube.com/watch?v=dYcvLw_jkkk

As we process this, we have to understand how we form our own opinions on the standard of righteousness. For instance, what is your life objective? Where do you believe you are or ought to be headed? Where do you want to go? Your answers to these questions are the foundation of what you think the world and the people in it ought to be. Family and cultural traditions are highly formative in the individual's worldview. That's why we are particularly influenced by our childhood – sometimes good, sometimes bad. As we grow older, we are inundated daily with societal messages and expectations from educational systems, politics, our peers, religious systems, media, etc. These messages inform a person's ideas of how you or I should be, but we have to ask ourselves the question, how many of these messages are trustworthy? They *all* fluctuate. Many would argue that my own opinions determine what is right for me. But there are eight billion opinions that are relative, will inevitably change, and will unavoidably conflict. If all humans have unique opinions, what determines who is right? How do you know something is right? The very concept of something being right assumes a standard. This is the question of humanity: is there a fixed, absolute, unchanging standard of what is right?

The very concept of something being right assumes a standard.

The Bureau of Weights and Measures establishes a standard. If I need a piece of wood three feet long, I have to measure it. I will roll out a measuring tape to determine a three-foot length, mark it, and cut it. Then I am confident that I have a three-foot piece of wood because I have measured that wood against something outside of my own opinion. This is why Sartre's statement, "No finite point has meaning without an infinite reference point," is a statement of despair. He is confessing that he has no meaning because there was no reference for humanity outside of himself. In his determination and understanding, the only thing he can know is himself, what he is thinking, what he is experiencing, and how he is feeling. Beyond his own knowledge and experience, he sees that there's no meaning.

Sincerity Does Not Make Something Right

> Opinion alone as my authority is self-reference. It is woefully short-sighted and has the logical consistency of saying that my car created itself.

A common argument is that what matters is the sincerity of my attitude at the time. But my sincerity does not determine the truthfulness of my positions, as I have limited understanding and perspective. Opinion alone as my authority is self-reference. It is woefully short-sighted and has the logical consistency of saying that my car created itself.

Francis Schaeffer can help us unpack this:

When as a Christian I bow before this God who is there, then I can move out of the only logical position which the non-Christian can hold. This is, the non-Christian must dwell consciously but silently in the cocoon of his being, without knowing anything outside of himself. This is the final dilemma of positivism on any variety. It is a hopeless situation.[4]

I might *have opinions about* what is outside myself, but I cannot *know* anything outside of myself. *Positivism* is a philosophical system which posits that any rational assertion can be logically, scientifically, or mathematically proven. It eliminates anything beyond the physical world that cannot be seen or empirically observed. Science can only observe that which can be repeated: observe, draw data, make conclusions – that is the scientific method. Anything outside of what can be observed is known as metaphysics. Because it only focuses on what can be observed, positivism writes off metaphysics – and of course any idea of theism. Positivism is a philosophical system that wipes God out of the picture. The bottom line is that the only reality for me is the reality that I know of myself. Schaeffer's assessment is correct: it is a hopeless situation.

---

[4] Francis Shaeffer, *True Spirituality*, (Tyndale House Publishers, Wheaton, IL,1971), p. 124

This is a hopeless conflict that cannot be resolved, because I am a finite and contingent being. I had a beginning, and I had nothing to do with it. Acknowledgment of that truth, combined with a belief that I cannot arrive at any meaningful purpose outside of what I determine presents a colossal problem. Through my own reasoning, I might arrive at what I believe is a meaningful purpose. But if I have done so while ignoring God (or believing that God does not exist), I have used God's gifts to arrive at that self-derived meaningful purpose. I have borrowed from God to arrive at this purpose, yet, there is nothing beyond that.

The prophet Isaiah states the outcome of self-reference: "All we like sheep have gone astray; we have turned – every one – to his own way" (Isaiah 53:6). As human sons and daughters of Adam, we are born with the problem of self-preeminence – the attitude and perspective that I am the greatest, most important reality, the center of my universe. Therefore, I view, perceive, and engage everything else in terms of how it relates to me. I demand you respect and affirm me, and I will pursue relationships only in terms of how they will benefit me. This is natural and problematic human behavior; as the prophet put it, "we have turned – every one – to his own way" – clearly a correct assessment on the condition of humanity.

The Place of Preeminence

Paul states a better and loftier objective in Colossians 1:18: "that in everything he [Christ] might be preeminent." This states how things ought to be.

> Identifying that infinite reference point is beyond the realm of mere human observation and discovery – it requires revelation.

The word *preeminent,* often understood as "first place", does not mean a place at the top of the list that is checked off before you go on with the rest of the list. Preeminent means the most important position at the center of everything. Like the hub of a wheel, everything revolves around it.

It is quite apparent that we desperately need righteousness! A reference point outside of ourselves – a standard of measurement – is necessary for the idea of righteousness to have any meaning. That reference point is not some entity at the Bureau of Weights and Measures. That entity is a person – the infinite creator, "for all his ways are justice" (Deuteronomy 32:4). He is our infinite reference point. Identifying that infinite reference point is beyond the realm of mere human observation and discovery – it requires revelation. As rational beings we can discover and recognize evidence of this reference point. We can acknowledge – even appreciate – his handiwork (Romans 1:20 and Psalm 19:1-6), but human reason alone cannot identify that infinite reference point.

As our master designer, God has established our purpose. We were created *for* him. When we are done with this life on earth, he is our destination. That makes him our reference point. That reality informs the "why?" of life; therefore, it informs us about how we should live – how we ought to be. Our reference point is the character and purpose of God as he has disclosed it. He is the standard of *right*. However, our inherent self-preeminence, handed down from our first parents, alienates us from God and causes us to depart from his righteous standard. That departure makes us unrighteous and makes it impossible for us to achieve righteousness regardless of how good we might think ourselves to be. We have become masters at comparing ourselves to each other, but when we compare ourselves to the standard, we find that we do not measure up. We have missed the mark, and we all "fall short of the glory of God" (Romans 3:23).

The Goodness of God

This perpetual missing of the mark is what makes the gospel what it is – good news. We are unrighteous and cannot achieve righteousness, "but now the righteousness of God has been manifested" (Romans 3:21). We desperately need a

> Just as darkness is not its own entity but is the absence of light, so unrighteousness is the absence of God in our lives.

righteousness that cannot be attained apart from what God has provided in the gospel of grace. For this reason, the disclosure of his character and purpose is necessary for us. He is holy, good, loving, gracious, kind, and forbearing. These are ways that we can – and must – become like him as we are called to be in Christ. Departure from God's character in our attitudes and behavior is sin; it is unrighteousness. Just as darkness is not its own entity but is the absence of light, so unrighteousness is the absence of God in our lives. Because God is infinite, he is everywhere; so how can we depart from him? It is the departure from God in my will, mind, and emotions that is unrighteousness. The question of *how I should be* is answered in how I measure up to God's character and purpose. When I depart from that, I am practicing unrighteousness in my life.

Isaiah's prophecy paints a clear contrast between the everlasting righteousness of God and the transience of unrighteous man:

> Lift up your eyes to the heavens and look at the earth beneath; for the heavens vanish like smoke, the earth will wear out like a garment, and they who dwell in it will die in like manner, but my salvation will be forever and my righteousness will never be dismayed. Listen to me, you who know righteousness, the people in whose heart is my law; fear not the reproach of man, nor

> be dismayed at their revilings. For the moth
> will eat them up like a garment, and the
> worm will eat them like wool, but my righ-
> teousness will be forever, and my salvation
> to all generations (Isaiah 51:6-8).

Every material thing created is temporal and will vanish in time; but the creator's character and purpose are an unchanging standard. God's holiness, love, justice, and grace are perfectly demonstrated in his purpose to reconcile mankind to himself for his glory and our good. When my life is aligned with that, I know and experience righteousness.

The Meaning of "Righteousness"

Let's look briefly at the biblical words for *righteousness*. The Hebrew word *sedeq* means conformity to a standard, what is correct, the right thing, and accurate. *Sedeq* is used in Genesis 15:6, "And he believed the Lord, and he counted it to him as righteousness," and Psalm 19:9, "the fear of the Lord is clean, enduring forever; the rules of the Lord are true, and righteous altogether." *Yasar* is another Hebrew word which means something, or someone is right, to go straight or direct in the way. *Yasar* is used in 2 Chronicles 20:32, "He walked in the way of Asa his father and did not turn aside from it, doing what was right in the sight of the Lord," and Psalm 19:8, "the precepts of the Lord are right, rejoicing the heart." The Greek word *dikaiosyne* means to be put right with. It is used in Matthew 25:46, "And these will go away into eternal punishment, but the righteous into eternal life," and Galatians 3:6, "just as Abraham 'believed God, and it was counted to him as righteousness.'"

If we are left to our own devices in our own efforts, righteousness is an unattainable ideal, which Paul points out in Romans 3:9-20. It is undeniable that human history bears this out as well. But the

Righteousness is attainable, but it cannot be achieved, only received.

gospel proclaims, "But now the righteousness of God has been manifested apart from the law, although the Law and the Prophets bear witness to it – the righteousness of God through faith in Jesus Christ for all who believe. For there is no distinction" (Romans 3:21-22). Righteousness is attainable, but it cannot be achieved, only received. 2 Corinthians 5:21 informs us of the source of the righteousness we so desperately need: "For our sake he made him [Christ] to be sin who knew no sin, so that in him we might become the righteousness of God." This is a profoundly comforting truth because what we need is righteousness. Righteousness is the core issue of the gospel. It is utterly unattainable on our own, but it is available to us through Jesus Christ.

The rest of this book will unpack what God does to make his righteousness available to us. God's righteousness is what we need to succeed at life – to realize our purpose, which is to know God and enjoy him forever.

Think About It

1. What comes to mind when we say that things in life are not the way they ought to be? What forces are in tension?

2. How does self-reference lead to interpersonal friction?

3. Why is conformity to a standard a distasteful concept to many?

4. In what way(s) might you be trusting your own righteous acts to gain God's approval?

CHAPTER 2

The Basis: **Propitiation**

A good and holy God must oppose evil.
He has dealt with our sin.

He is the propitiation for our sins.
1 John 2:2

It is better for you that one man should die for the
people, not that the whole nation should perish.
Caiaphas

T he first three chapters of Romans paint a portrait
of humanity that shows mankind has a problem:
we are an unrighteous people at the core.

> As it is written: "None is righteous, no, not
> one; no one understands; no one seeks for
> God. All have turned aside; together they
> have become worthless; no one does good,
> not even one." "Their throat is an open grave;
> they use their tongues to deceive." "The

venom of asps is under their lips." "Their mouth is full of curses and bitterness." "Their feet are swift to shed blood; in their paths are ruin and misery, and the way of peace they have not known." "There is no fear of God before their eyes" (Romans 3:10-18).

The knowledge of God is available for humanity, but we are blocking it; therefore, we do not understand God. That fittingly brings us to Paul's conclusion in Romans 3:20: "For by works of the law no human being will be justified in his sight, since through the law comes knowledge of sin." The law is a moral code. There is no behavior of man that will justify him before God, which is our problem of unrighteousness. We cannot be good enough to attain the standard of God's holiness. The good news is our story does not end there, as Paul dives into the depths of the gospel in verses 21-22: "But now the righteousness of God has been manifested apart from the law…the righteousness of God through faith in Jesus Christ for all who believe."

Loving Boundaries

Laws are for our good and our protection. Because God is righteous and good, he created us with loving boundaries. Even though Adam and Eve were

> **Because God is righteous and good, he created us with loving boundaries.**

20

surrounded by so much good in the garden of Eden, there was still a loving boundary: "Of the tree of the knowledge of good and evil you shall not eat, for in the day that you eat of it you shall surely die" (Genesis 2:17). Essentially, God said, "Here is a boundary that you should not cross, because I do not want you to engage in self-destructive behavior."

I was raised as a missionary kid in Colombia, South America. I loved the freedom to roam that my family had. We enjoyed many memorable outdoor experiences like hiking and mountain climbing. We would pitch a tent in view and earshot of a waterfall, start a fire, and camp overnight. Not wanting that to end when we came back to America, our family visited some of the national parks, including the Grand Canyon. We came upon a scenic overlook, separated from majestic cliffs by a road-side fence. Dad stopped the car and we kids enthusiastically jumped out, ready to roam. We immediately climbed the fence to get a good look at the precipice. We thought nothing of the danger below, but the park ranger was suddenly preoccupied with our behavior! We saw the fence as an obstacle to our exploration, rather than a boundary for our safety. God's boundaries are part of his love for us. If there were no boundaries, then we would run headlong into destruction.

> God's boundaries are part of his love for us. If there were no boundaries, then we would run headlong into destruction.

When I was a youth pastor in Virginia, we used the labor of church members to build a gymnasium. During the drawn-out endeavor, our church used the finished part of the gym while other sections were still under construction. On one occasion at a family event, a father pointedly instructed his child: "Son, do you see that line? Do not cross that, because on the other side there is danger, and you could get hurt. You may not go over there. Stay on this side of the line." Upon receiving those instructions, the little boy proceeded to walk all the way across the floor following the do-not-cross line while looking at the other side. It seemed clear to me what was occupying his young mind: "Let me see what I'm missing out on." These examples reflect the nature of man's trespass. I John 3:4 says that "sin is lawlessness." *Lawlessness* simply means the ambition to cross over God's boundaries.

The Revolution Within

Lawlessness is the problem in the heart of every person. The origin of lawlessness is recorded in Isaiah 14:12-14:

> When we take our focus off God and focus on ourselves, we become preoccupied with our own limits.

"How you are fallen from heaven,
  O Day Star, son of Dawn!
  How you are cut down to
    the ground,

you who laid the nations low!
You said in your heart,
'I will ascend to heaven;
above the stars of God
I will set my throne on high;
I will sit on the mount of assembly
in the far reaches of the north;
I will ascend above the heights of the clouds;
I will make myself like the Most High.'"

When we take our focus off God and focus on ourselves, we become preoccupied with our own limits. One of the chief tactics of the adversary is to take our focus off of God by tempting us with what we do not have; then, we invest our resources and energy in obtaining it. This is how he tempted Adam and Eve at the very beginning in the garden.

God's loving boundaries are for our protection; sin happens when we cross over those boundaries. Just like Adam and Eve, we are trespassers, and our sin separates us from God. We have gone contrary to his holy character, and such behavior can only destroy us. Our separation from God is necessary. Just as a single drop of the lethal toxin ricin would contaminate a gallon of purified water, so our sin is like a drop of deadly poison in the pure water of God's perfect nature. God's absolute perfection cannot coexist with evil because God is holy. Our sin makes our separation from God necessary, in the same way that impurities should be kept separate from purified water. The difference is that God's holiness is not water, but rather a consuming fire. Were we to encounter God, he would not be tainted — we would be consumed.

This concept of separation from God might seem to contradict Psalm 139:8: "If I ascend to heaven, you are there! If I make my bed in Sheol, you are there!" One of God's attributes is his omnipresence; it is not possible to be somewhere where God is not present. So how can we be separated from God

> The presence of God for those who are spiritually separated from him is incinerating.

by our sin since we cannot be anywhere that God is not present? As Paul said to the Athenians, "In him we live and move and have our being" (Acts 17:28). God is infinite and transcends all the created order. Remember how we mentioned that God is a consuming fire (Hebrews 12:29)? The presence of God for those who are spiritually separated from him is incinerating. He is not refreshment – that satisfaction of love, joy, and peace – but a fire that consumes. We are utterly alone and destitute with no resource, "dying" of thirst. When Christ was on the cross, paying for your sin and mine, he cried out to his Father: "My God, my God, why have you forsaken me?" (Matthew 27:46). Though God is omnipresent, there was no loving fellowship, only a necessary holy rejection. This is why the Bible uses the picture of God turning his back on his only begotten Son. This is the same separation that will be true in eternity for those who are spiritually separated from the One who is the Giver and Sustainer of life.

Appeasement

The sinfulness at the core of our being separates us from an infinitely holy God. This alienation from God is the fundamental problem of humanity. The basic question, then, is this: How can unrighteous humans be reconciled to a holy God? We cannot find it in ourselves; we cannot do enough to attain the righteous standard of God's holiness. This is where Paul, speaking of Christ, introduces us to the word *propitiation* in Romans 3:25: "whom God put forward as a propitiation by his blood." The root idea of the word *propitiation* is appeasement. In Greek mythology, the gods needed to be appeased because they were much like humans in their emotional disposition. In most religious systems, people devote a colossal amount of time and resources to appeasing the divine in order not to suffer wrath. For example, three mummified Inca children were discovered in a South American excavation site that had been sacrificed to their deity during a famine. The Incas believed the gods were angry, so they sacrificed their children to appease the gods so that rain would come.[5] This is a common pattern of false religions – appeasement merits divine favor.

---

[5] http://news.bbc.co.uk/1/hi/sci/tech/312846.stm

However, the biblical use of the term *propitiation* turns this concept on its head. Genesis 3:22-24 states,

> Then the Lord God said, "Behold, the man has become like one of us in knowing good and evil. Now, lest he reach out his hand and take also of the tree of life and eat, and live forever—" therefore the Lord God sent him out from the garden of Eden to work the ground from which he was taken. He drove out the man, and at the east of the garden of Eden he placed the cherubim and a flaming sword that turned every way to guard the way to the tree of life.

The first humans in the garden of Eden joyfully experienced God's presence. When they trespassed God's loving boundary, he put them out of the garden and placed cherubim with flaming swords at the gate to prohibit re-entry. This separation was the moment they experienced death. God said, "in the day that you eat of it you shall surely die." On that day, there was a spiritual death as well as the introduction to the physical corruption that would ultimately lead to physical death. The physical separation that God imposed on Adam and Eve was to protect them – and us – from perpetual separation from God. God was communicating, "Keep out. You cannot come to me." We know, however, from the gospel story that God would also say, "I will come to you and make provision, so you can be reconciled to me."

Removing the Obstacle

Under the Mosaic law, the ark of the covenant sat in the holy place behind the veil in the temple. The top of the ark was made of gold; inside the ark there were meaningful reminders of God's covenant with his people. The lid of the ark is called the *mercy seat* (Exodus 37:9). In the Septuagint, the Greek translation of the Old Testament, the word for *mercy seat* was translated *hilastērion*, which is the same Greek word Paul used in Romans 3:25 for *propitiation*. The ark contained the law—the boundaries that they continually trespassed. The book of Hebrews points out clearly that the law served one chief purpose: to remind them that they were a sinful, unrighteous people, necessarily separated from holy God (for example see Hebrews 10:3). Approaching God now required the forfeiture of life because of sin. God instructed that once a year, on the Day of Atonement, the high priest go in behind the veil and sprinkle the mercy seat with blood (see Leviticus 16). God said of the mercy seat: "There I will meet with you."

Let's look at the description of the mercy seat from Exodus 25:20-22:

God said of the mercy seat: "There I will meet with you."

> The cherubim shall spread out their wings above, overshadowing the mercy seat with their wings, their faces one to another; toward the mercy seat shall the faces of the cherubim be. And you shall put the mercy seat on the top of the ark, and in the ark you shall put the testimony that I shall give you. There I will meet with you, and from above the mercy seat, from between the two cherubim that are on the ark of the testimony, I will speak with you about all that I will give you in commandment for the people of Israel.

This central piece of temple furniture held powerful imagery for the people. The veil represented the warning: "Keep out." The two cherubim represented something God did not want people to forget: "Remember the cherubim that were placed at the garden with flaming swords? If you try to approach, it is to your destruction; you cannot come to God – separation is necessary." The shed blood represented the necessary loss of the sacrificed life, which provided a temporary covering for sin.

"Behold, the Lamb of God, who takes away the sin of the world!"

Every year when the sacrifice was made, the high priest *alone* went behind the curtain to sprinkle blood on the mercy seat. The high priest's actions represented God's forbearance "to show God's righteousness, because in his divine forbearance he had passed over former sins" (Romans 3:25b). All the high priest was sprinkling was the blood of an animal; there was no way that animal life could pay for, or atone for, the sin of humanity. This forbearance takes us back to God's infinite and transcendent perspective, his omniscience. As God led his people, these things – the ark of the covenant, the animal sacrifice, the sprinkling of blood – were a foreshadowing of the perfect sacrifice that would come in Jesus Christ.

This gives meaning to John the Baptist's words publicly introducing Jesus: "Behold, the Lamb of God, who takes away the sin of the world!" (John 1:29). In Hebrews, the writer builds upon the foreshadowing of the Levitical sacrificial system to show that Jesus Christ, in the work that he accomplished, was the perfect fulfillment of God's requirements for his people. I John 3:8 says, "The reason the Son of God appeared was to destroy the works of the devil." The work of the devil is our ambition to trespass God's loving boundaries that results in separation from him. That is why John says, "the whole world lies in the power of the evil one" (1 John 5:19).

Sacrifice

Here is how all of this is woven together. God, in his infinite love and holiness, necessarily had to deal with sin. If God did not deal with sin, he would not be good, and he would not be God. He could not just overlook sin. In his goodness, he was unwilling to leave a destructive force unchecked. There was no remedy in mankind; the only remedy was in himself. So, he gave himself – he demonstrated his grace. God came to us in the person of his Son who lived a perfect human life. Upon his death on the cross, he took the massive strike of God's holy, necessary wrath – that is *propitiation*.

> If God did not deal with sin, he would not be good, and he would not be God.

Let's re-examine the imagery and reality of *propitiation*. In the Old Testament sacrificial system, the mercy seat and the sprinkled blood represented the forfeiture of life. When Jesus died on the cross, the forfeiture of his life was not just a *physical* death. He also experienced *propitiatory* death when he was relationally separated from his Father. As stated previously, the lid of the ark is called the *mercy seat*, and the Greek translation of *mercy seat* is the same word used in the New Testament for *propitiation*. Propitiation means that God poured out his wrath on what separates us from him – our sin. He removed our sin by providing satisfaction (appeasement) for the broken law. At the

> Propitiation means that God poured out his wrath on what separates us from him – our sin.

moment Jesus cried out, "My God, my God, why have you forsaken me?" (Mark 15:34), Jesus took the punishment that we deserve and absorbed the wrath of God in himself. Again, why would God do this? Because a holy God must deal with sin. In the act of the cross, we see not only his judgment but also his boundless love. He did this for us because he wants us to be with him. Remember what God said to Moses as he was giving the instructions for the mercy seat: "There I will meet with you." Because of the sacrifice that Christ made when he took God's wrath for me, God now looks at me and says, "There I will meet with you." This is only possible because, as Romans 3:25 says, "whom God put forward as a propitiation by his blood." God can only meet with us based on the forfeiture of Christ's life and the fact that the Father turned his back on the Son, taking the full measure of God's wrath that you and I deserve.

Substitute

2 Corinthians 5:21 says, "For our sake he made him to be sin who knew no sin…." He was qualified to do this because he was perfect and without sin. Why did he do this? "…so that in him we might become the righteousness of God." When Jesus was on the cross, one of his last words was *tetelestai* – translated "It is finished!" The Greek word *tetelestai* means paid in full! When Jesus uttered that declaration, the righteous demand of

God's holiness was fully met because Jesus Christ experienced God's necessary wrath in our place. He took it for us so that we could live.

We are an unrighteous people; we are evil at the core. So how can unrighteousness be brought together with perfect holiness? The two cannot come together unless justice has been satisfactorily met. God set forth Jesus as a propitiation by His blood. "He made him to be sin who knew no sin, so that in him we might become the righteousness of God" – we become righteousness! The basis for this righteousness is propitiation: Jesus took the necessary blow of God's wrath in himself so that we could receive the righteousness that God requires. Then God says, "There I will meet with you." 2 Corinthians 5:19-21 states,

> In Christ God was reconciling the world to himself, not counting their trespasses against them, and entrusting to us the message of reconciliation. Therefore, we are ambassadors for Christ, God making his appeal through us. We implore you on behalf of Christ, be reconciled to God. For our sake he made him to be sin who knew no sin, so that in him we might become the righteousness of God.

Jesus became sin *for* us. It was his divinity – the essence of infinitude – and his perfect life that qualified him to meet the righteous requirement of God's holiness. His perfect divine life was sacrificed. Think about that! In his perfection, he suffered separation from God – God's wrath – for us. He made it possible for us to receive the righteousness of God, therefore God can say, "Now I can meet you." Our caustic, evil nature

> **In his perfection, he suffered separation from God – God's wrath – for us.**

of unrighteousness has been neutralized, and we can once again draw near to God on the sole basis of Jesus' shed blood on the mercy seat – he is our propitiation. The writer of Hebrews invites us saying, "Let us draw near with a true heart in full assurance of faith" (Hebrews 10:22). Because God has come to us, and through his Son met the demands of his holiness, we can now draw near to him. Hear him saying, "There I will meet with you."

Jesus freely humbled himself to death on the cross for our success. I define *success* as "living according to design" or "realized purpose." God created us to enjoy him in loving fellowship with him. For this to be possible, propitiation was necessary. Apart from propitiation, the only thing we could experience is the just judgment of God.

The wonder of propitiation may have been on the mind of Charles Wesley when he wrote the great hymn, "And Can It Be?"

Amazing love! how can it be
That Thou, my God, shouldst die for me!

This wonderful contemplation is the gospel of grace, and there is nothing else like it in the universe! God took the initiative to provide this propitiation so we can realize our purpose as human beings created in his image. We are created *by* God and *for* God, so it is a profoundly beautiful thing to know that God has said, "I will meet with you."

Think About It

1. From what you know of mythology or religion, identify how humans seeking favor attempt to appease the divine.

2. What are instances where some question if God opposes evil?

3. Give examples where one sacrifices for the welfare of another.

4. Put in your own words how far God would go so that you could meet with him?

CHAPTER 3

The Cost: **Redemption**

Bought back and set free at an enormous price.

The redemption that is in Christ Jesus
Romans 3:24

Human history is the long terrible story of
man trying to find something other than
God which will make him happy.
C.S. Lewis

I magine being in a loving relationship with one who cares for, protects, accepts, and draws you to himself continually. This relationship has no inhibitors and no pretense — only a strong sense of belonging, security, and meaning, but something distracts you and lures you to believe that he's holding out on you. This loving relationship is only keeping you back from enjoying something more — more pleasure, more satisfaction. You break it off diving into other relationships that seem to be more pleasurable but end up being oppressive, enslaving, and ultimately destructive. You have been sold and exploited.

This is the summation of the historical narrative in the first three chapters of Genesis. In the garden of Eden, Adam and Eve walked with God in a loving, joyful relationship. Then, the tempter convinced them that God was holding out on them. God's confines were not loving boundaries, but imposing limits keeping them from enjoying greater experience and pleasure. Genesis 3:6 reads like the first commercial of history:

> So when the woman saw that the tree was good for food, and that it was a delight to the eyes, and that the tree was to be desired to make one wise, she took of its fruit and ate, and she also gave some to her husband who was with her, and he ate.

Selfish Ambition

Why would God put a prohibition in the context of perfection? Why plant the Tree of the Knowledge of Good and Evil in the middle of the garden and allow Satan to enter the garden to tempt Eve? To better understand this, we must go back before the pivotal moment in

How absurd it is that a created being thinks he can exalt himself above the Creator! That is the irrational nature of sin.

paradise. Satan fell from his exalted position as a beautiful messenger of God before he entered the garden as the tempter. His sin of pride and his unrighteousness of self-focus as described in Isaiah 14:12-15 was discussed in chapter two. How absurd it is that a created being thinks he can exalt himself above the Creator! That is the irrational nature of sin.

The created being is inherently limited, for something created cannot be infinite. The prophet Ezekiel gives us a glimpse into the rebel's mind:

> "You were in Eden, the garden of God; every precious stone was your covering, sardius, topaz, and diamond, beryl, onyx, and jasper, sapphire, emerald, and carbuncle; and crafted in gold were your settings and your engravings. On the day that you were created they were prepared. You were an anointed guardian cherub. I placed you; you were on the holy mountain of God; in the midst of the stones of fire you walked. You were blameless in your ways from the day you were created, till unrighteousness was found in you. In the abundance of your trade you were filled with violence in your midst, and you sinned; so I cast you as a profane thing from the mountain of God, and I destroyed you, O guardian cherub, from the midst of the stones of fire. Your

heart was proud because of your beauty; you corrupted your wisdom for the sake of your splendor. I cast you to the ground; I exposed you before kings, to feast their eyes on you" (Ezekiel 28:13–17).

This deceiver began as a beautiful cherub of high position until unrighteousness was found in him. His unrighteousness began when he shifted his focus from his glorious creator and contemplated himself. In his self-focus, he became dissatisfied with his place and his limits; therefore, self-preoccupation led him to devastating ambition. Having been cast out "from the mountain of God," he approached Adam and Eve enjoying the perfect environment of the garden of Eden.

Our adversary, the devil, is "like a roaring lion, seeking someone to devour" (1 Peter 5:8). His ambition from the dawn of human history has been to consume whomever he can for his pleasure – this is the essence of living for self. We have sold ourselves to a master who only wants to devour us instead of living in submission to the loving, benevolent Creator who alone sustains and satisfies us. Adam and Eve recognized that something had gone terribly

> We have sold ourselves to a master who only wants to devour us instead of living in submission to the loving, benevolent Creator who alone sustains and satisfies us.

wrong after they encroached upon God's boundary. By making this decision, they had severed themselves from their source of joy and satisfaction. According to Paul, as their descendants, we are born with a sinful nature, but also an understanding of God because we are made in his image.

> For what can be known about God is plain to them, because God has shown it to them. For his invisible attributes, namely, his eternal power and divine nature, have been clearly perceived, ever since the creation of the world, in the things that have been made. So they are without excuse (Romans 1:19-20).

However, we are also born with a natural bent to suppress that understanding and pursue our own ambitions and pleasures apart from him, thinking we know better than he does. Our sinful human nature enslaves us – we are held hostage by our self-centered rebellion. That rebellion separates us from God, selling us into slavery and placing us under the curse of the law. The law is a reminder of the debt to the holiness of God that we cannot satisfy. Our self-preeminence is the evidence that we are mastered by – "in the power of" – the control of darkness (1 John 5:19).

The Test of Love

We must understand these events in light of God's perfect goodness toward us. God does not need evil to accomplish his purpose. God's love compelled him to create rational, volitional beings in his likeness who could fully benefit from and delight in his perfect goodness. Every person created in the image of God is inherently valuable, as we were made *by* him and *for* him. We were created with the design and intent to know God and relate to him in satisfaction and delight. This is the criteria for what we call *success* – functioning according to God's design and realizing our highest purpose, which is to know God and to love him.

> We were created with the design and intent to know God and relate to him in satisfaction and delight.

But for love to *be* love, it must be free and spontaneous, based on the commitment and delight of the one loving toward the one loved. Love cannot be designed, programmed, demanded, or coerced. The Tree of the Knowledge of Good and Evil in the garden of Eden was the sole prohibition in a context of perfection. It was God's test of love: "Do you love me?" Adam and Eve chose to love themselves instead. That natural bent has been handed down to us as their rebel descendants. Every little child born as a human being is created in the image of God and wonderfully made in God's sovereign purpose. That wonderful little package of love and joy is also a child of Adam and Eve, and therefore a rebel. We don't need to teach our children to sin – to be selfish or to get outraged when they do not get their way. They sin because they are sinners by nature.

The trespass by our first parents in the garden made as much sense as a tree branch desiring freedom from the tree. Those God created for loving, satisfying delight have rebelled against him and are now held hostage by their own rebellion. As a result, we desperately need rescue from the bondage of our self-preeminence, the power of darkness, and the path of destruction. We need redemption because we have a debt that we could never pay – a debt to the righteousness of God.

Our redemption in Christ means our debt is paid in full. Christ paid our ransom by pro-pitiation – he suffered the full intensity of God's wrath that we deserve. Romans 3:24 states that we have been "justified by his grace as a gift, through the redemption that is in Christ Jesus." Religions other than the gospel of grace teach that you must do something to appease the divine. This appeasement will earn you the favor of the divine – or at least keep them from oppressing you. Conversely, the biblical gospel teaches us that God himself provided the appeasement (propitiation) of his necessary, holy wrath that we deserve. *Redemption* means he has paid

> We have revolted against the Creator who is our source and our sustainer.

the ransom for us. Jesus states, "the Son of Man came not to be served but to serve, and to give his life as a ransom for many" (Matthew 20:28). Paul also asserts, "who gave himself as a ransom for all" (1 Timothy 2:6). To whom has Jesus paid the ransom? The word *ransom* makes us think of somebody that has been kidnapped, but we are not just victims. We have revolted against the Creator who is our source and our sustainer. This theme stands out in the Old Testament: the curtain veiling the holiest place in the temple represents the necessary separation between sinful man and holy God. We are broken off from God in a way that we cannot remedy.

Nuances

There are two Greek words that are used for *redemption* in Scripture. The first is *exagorazo*, which means to buy back (1 Corinthians 6:20; Galatians 3:13). We are held hostage by our own selfish ambitions — swayed by the luring treachery of the master deceiver, the agent of our enslavement. John describes this deception as a global reality: "The whole world lies in the power of the evil one" (1 John 5:19). Paul also contrasts those who are dead in sin versus those who are alive in Christ: "You were dead in the trespasses and sins…" (Ephesians 2:1-3). But we are bought back; we are redeemed. The second word, *apolutrosis*, means to release upon payment of ransom (Ephesians 1:7; Hebrews 9:11). The biblical doctrine of redemption conveys the meanings of both words: *exagorazo* – to buy back, paying that debt to the holiness of God; and then *apolutrosis* – to release upon payment of ransom.

Two Prepositions

To further understand these two senses in the doctrine of redemption, it will help us to consider the prepositions: redemption *from*, and redemption (or release) *to*. God's supreme act of love, the cross of Christ, was a powerful, destructive force that released us *from* the claws of sin's oppressive grip. This redemption then releases us *to* the life that God intended and designed for us. "He has delivered us *from* the domain of darkness and transferred us *to* the kingdom of his beloved Son, in whom we have *redemption*, the forgiveness of sins" (Colossians 1:13–14, emphasis added). This "domain of darkness" refers to the Accuser, the Deceiver, the Father of Lies; this adversary of our souls is also called "the god of this world" (2 Corinthians 4:4) because the world lies under his sway. He has the deceptive power of death – our separation from God – so he can consume us for his pleasure. Christ's propitiation pays the ransom to rescue us from the domain of the one who has this power (Hebrews 2:14).

Redeemed *from*

The Screwtape Letters, written by C. S. Lewis, imagines a senior demon named Screwtape instructing a junior demon on demonic activity through letters. Screwtape always refers to Christ as "the enemy." In his introduction to the book, Lewis posits his view of the realm of demons and those in their bondage:

We must picture Hell as a state where everyone is perpetually concerned about his own dignity and advancement, where everyone has a grievance, and where everyone lives the deadly serious passion of envy, self-importance, and resentment.[6]

> But there the hunger is more ravenous, and a fuller satisfaction is possible. There, I suggest, the stronger spirit …can really and irrevocably suck the weaker into itself and permanently gorge its own being on the weaker's outraged individuality. It is (I feign) for this that devils desire human souls and the souls of one another. It is for this that Satan desires all his own followers and all the sons of Eve and all the host of heaven. His dream is of the day when all shall be inside him and all that says, I, can say it only through him.[7]

Lewis gives a grim description of this roaring lion who seeks prey to devour for his own pleasure. He

---

[6] C. S. Lewis, *The Screwtape Letters*, (The MacMillan Company, New York, 1971) p. ix

[7] C.S. Lewis, *The Screwtape Letters*, p. xi -xii

wants to consume us through our desires; we are led away by our passions – we pursue what we desire. From the beginning of humanity, our first parents were distracted and led away by their appetite for what they were deceived to believe was more than what God had to offer. A person not in Christ is held captive by that powerful deception. We need rescue – we need redemption; we need to be bought back to be released from this power of darkness and the path of destruction. We find that path described by James:

> Let no one say when he is tempted, "I am being tempted by God," for God cannot be tempted with evil, and he himself tempts no one. But each person is tempted when he is lured and enticed by his own desire. Then desire when it has conceived gives birth to sin, and sin, when it is fully grown brings forth death (James 1:13-15).

We need rescue because Scripture tells us, "the wages of sin is death…" (Romans 6:23). That is the curse of the law, the necessary separation from God – his wrath – from which we desperately need saving. Christ's redemption rescues us *from* the power of darkness *and* the wrath of God. In Christ's redemption, we have the forgiveness of sins. Forgiveness means absorbing a debt, and Christ has absorbed our debt (Colossians 2:14).

Released *to*

Redemption is also the reality that we are released *to* what our Creator intended for us from the beginning. "And he died for all, that those who live might no longer live for themselves but for him who for their sake died and was raised" (2 Corinthians 5:15). We are released from the power of darkness and the path of destruction; then, we are liberated to live for him. He has not rescued us to live autonomous lives. That would be akin to removing us from one form of slavery and putting us in another. He rescues us to live according to our design – to realize our purpose – because we were made for him and designed to enjoy him. We were created with the inherent purpose of serving him with delight as our loving, benevolent sovereign. We are liberated to restoration to that relationship for which we were designed thereby finding satisfaction in him. C.S. Lewis well describes that *to which* we are liberated in this redemption:

> We are released from the power of darkness and the path of destruction; then, we are liberated to live for him.

> [This is] that unfathomed bounty whereby God turns tools into servants and servants into sons, so that they may be at last reunited to him in the perfect freedom of a love offered from the height of the utter

individualities which he has liberated them to be.[8]

God created us as individuals in his image and he created us with a lofty purpose. Now when we are dead in sin, we are held hostage by our rebellion in the domain of darkness on the path of destruction. The redemption of Christ rescues us from bondage and wrath and releases us to love and delight in him and thereby find the purpose and satisfaction for which we were created. He did not just purchase us back; he released us to be reunited with him in the perfect freedom of the love for which he created us. Augustine summed it up accurately in his confession, "You awakened us to delight in Your praise for You made us for Yourself, and our heart is restless until it finds its rest in You."[9]

> The redemption of Christ rescues us from bondage and wrath and releases us to love and delight in him and thereby find the purpose and satisfaction for which we were created.

Through redemption, we are released *to* this loving relationship with God. That is why reconciliation that is based upon Christ's propitiation and redemption is necessary. The death of this one counts for all unrighteousness, but how does Christ make one righteous before

---

[8] C.S. Lewis, *The Screwtape Letters*, p. xii

[9] Augustine, *The Confessions*, 1:1

God? That is what we will discover in the doctrine of *imputation*.

Think About It

1. If passions are natural, how can they be evil?

2. How can a person be held hostage by their desires?

3. What is the nature of the debt that was paid at the cross of Christ?

4. Why is it important to understand that redemption is not just liberation *from*, but liberation *to*?

CHAPTER 4

The Means: **Imputation**

How the action of one is experienced by the many.

It will be counted to us who believe
Romans 4:24

Many think if they give a penny to a pardoner,
they shall be forgiven the breaking of all
the commandments of God, and therefore
they take no heed how they keep them.
John Wycliff

B ased on the propitiation and redemption that
Christ accomplished on the cross, the doctrine of
imputation becomes possible. Paul makes a distinction
between the religion of grace and all other religions of
merit whereby the person earns acceptance by god(s).
These merit-based religions are part of our fallen human
nature which feels the need for redemption and forgiveness and the need to make ourselves worthy again. We
seek some way to appease the higher power or to make

things right with the cosmos. These religions are crafted from human reason, passion, and imagination. There is but one gospel of grace.

Examples from the Old Testament

Paul uses two examples of the doctrine of imputation from the Old Testament which eliminate all possibility of boasting that one can earn acceptance before God. Here is the premise:

> Then what becomes of our boasting? It is excluded. By what kind of law? By a law of works? No, but by the law of faith. For we hold that one is justified by faith apart from works of the law (Romans 3:27–28).

Let's look at the examples of imputation that he gives in Romans 4:

> What then shall we say was gained by Abraham, our forefather according to the flesh? For if Abraham was justified by works, he has something to boast about, but not before God. For what does the Scripture say? "Abraham believed God, and it was counted to him as righteousness" (Romans 4:1-3).

The word *counted* is a Greek word often translated to English as *imputed*. Abraham's lack of righteousness was remedied by faith. We need righteousness, but we cannot attain it on our own; it must be credited, counted, *imputed* to us. It cannot be achieved; it must be received.

> For what does the Scripture say? "Abraham believed God, and it was counted to him as righteousness." Now to the one who works, his wages are not counted as a gift but as his due. And to the one who does not work but believes in him who justifies the ungodly, his faith is counted as righteousness, just as David also speaks of the blessing of the one to whom God counts righteousness apart from works: "Blessed are those whose lawless deeds are forgiven, and whose sins are covered; blessed is the man against whom the Lord will not count his sin" (Romans 4:3–8).

Abraham was credited with righteousness by faith *before* the law of Moses. Paul makes it clear that Abraham could not have obtained righteousness by doing the works of the law (measuring up to a standard of morality) because he preceded the law.

> For the promise to Abraham and his offspring that he would be heir of the world

did not come through the law but through the righteousness of faith. For if it is the adherents of the law who are to be the heirs, faith is null and the promise is void. For the law brings wrath, but where there is no law there is no transgression. That is why it depends on faith, in order that the promise may rest on grace and be guaranteed to all his offspring — not only to the adherent of the law but also to the one who shares the faith of Abraham, who is the father of us all (Romans 4:13–16).

God, "who gives life to the dead and calls into existence the things that do not exist" (v.17), made a promise to Abraham. Abraham placed his faith in God: "in hope he believed against hope, that he should become the father of many nations, as he had been told, 'So shall your offspring be'" (v. 18). The Scripture says "against hope" because God promised Abraham that he would father a great nation. But there was a problem – he and his wife were well beyond child-bearing age. Contrary to any mere human hope or expectation that an heir would be born, God made a promise. The important point of this example is not *how much* faith Abraham expressed, but rather the *object* of his faith. Abraham believed the God who is sovereign over creation and had promised, "I will make of you a great nation" (Genesis 12:2).

He did not weaken in faith when he considered his own body, which was as good as
dead (since he was about a hundred years
old), or when he considered the barrenness
of Sarah's womb. No unbelief made him
waver concerning the promise of God, but
he grew strong in his faith as he gave glory
to God, fully convinced that God was able
to do what he had promised (Romans 4:19-21).

Faith is clearly defined in the above text: "fully convinced that God was able to do what he had promised.
That is why his faith was 'counted to him as righteousness'" (vv. 21-22).

But the words "it was counted to him" were
not written for his sake alone, but for ours
also. [Righteousness] will be *counted to us
who believe in him* who raised from the dead
Jesus our Lord, who was delivered up for
our trespasses and raised for our justification (Romans 4:23-25 emphasis added).

Righteousness Through Faith

Four millennia ago, faith was counted as righteousness for Abraham; the same is true for us today. The
Greek word for *counted* or *imputed* is *logizomai*, an eco-
nomic term which means to take inventory or to pass

one's account. It was a common term among tax collectors and accountants. Michael Horton provides us with a good personal illustration:

> After my junior year in college, I went to Europe with some friends. Having misjudged my expenses by several digits, I phoned home for help. My parents transferred money from their account to cover outstanding bills and included an additional sum from which I could draw until the end of the trip.
>
> **Imputation is transferring credited righteousness from an infinite account to a limited account; from God, who has infinite righteousness, to you and me, who have none.**
>
> Now, was this money, which I was going to draw daily as I needed, strictly speaking, *my* money? No, it belonged to my parents; nevertheless, because they had transferred it to my account, it was my money. My account was now filled with money I had not earned but which was mine to use nonetheless.[10]

---

[10] Michael Horton, *Putting the Amazing Back into Grace* (Baker, 2010), pp. 148-155

Imputation is transferring credited righteousness from an infinite account to a limited account; from God, who has infinite righteousness, to you and me, who have none.

David also speaks of this idea of imputation.

> Blessed is the one whose transgression is forgiven, whose sin is covered. Blessed is the man against whom the Lord counts no iniquity (Psalm 32:1-2).

We have an amazing God who stands ready to forgive because the debt has been paid by the propitiation and redemption that Jesus Christ accomplished on the cross.

Forgiveness is the release of a debt – payment is no longer required. If I have been forgiven, I owed a debt that has now been absorbed (propitiation) by the one who has forgiven me. Sin is no longer credited to my account – it is not held against me. God has paid my ransom (redemption). 2 Corinthians 5:19 is an amazing verse that ties this all together! "In Christ God was reconciling the world to himself, not counting their trespasses against them." We have an amazing God who stands ready to forgive because the debt has been paid by the propitiation and redemption that Jesus Christ accomplished on the cross.

Man cannot earn the righteousness of God. It must come through faith, that it might be according to grace (God's investment) apart from the law (Romans 3:21-22). It must be a righteousness that is imputed (credited) to the unrighteous creature's account. It cannot be our righteousness; it must be his.

Paul, who at one time was a self-righteous religious leader, affirms and celebrates this:

> But whatever gain I had, I counted as loss for the sake of Christ. Indeed, I count everything as loss because of the surpassing worth of knowing Christ Jesus my Lord. For his sake I have suffered the loss of all things and count them as rubbish, in order that I may gain Christ and be found in him, not having a righteousness of my own that comes from the law, but that which comes through faith in Christ, the righteousness from God that depends on faith (Philippians 3:7-9).

The previous examples of David and Abraham show they were imputed righteousness because they believed in God as he revealed himself to them. Their righteousness was of faith that it might be according to grace. It is apart from rituals and requirements and it's not a transaction of wages or debt. Even though righteousness is something credited and received, that does not mean that we owe God. That would put our righteousness back into the category of merit, a sort of *quid pro quo*. It is not in any way earned; it is utterly impossible for us to pay it back.

From One to Many

Now let's consider how righteousness is credited and received. The word for *faith* (*pisteuo*) is often translated "to entrust" (Luke 16:11; John 2:24; Romans 3:2; Galatians 2:7; Titus 1:3). When a human encounters and submits to God's self-disclosure, I call it "surrendered trust." Truly, the only appropriate response to sovereignty is surrender. We misunderstand faith when we assume that faith means conforming to a particular moral system, adopting a formal creed, or behaving a certain way without evidence or reason. For example, years ago, a local news cast reported that a young woman was missing, and the community banded together to form a search party. One member of the search party, while interviewed by a reporter, said, "I believe we are going to find her." She did not base that *belief* upon any specific information or evidence. It was little more than wishful thinking. Faith is also commonly perceived as nothing more than a spiritualized form of positive thinking. We may also accept the popular notion that faith and reason are mutually exclusive. These are natural, human ideas about the concept of faith, none of which can attain righteousness for us. Paul demolished these perceptions, instead showing us examples of true faith that result in imputed, credited righteousness.

When Abraham and David entrusted themselves to the promises (information) and grace (actions) of God, they were credited with Christ's righteousness. God created us in his image, which includes our capacity to relate to him. I would like to point out, we cannot entrust ourselves to information (God's promises) without exercising reason but let me be clear: human reason *alone* cannot lead us to the knowledge of God **We must base our faith in true information – the self-disclosure of God.** that will redeem us and reconcile us to him. We must base our faith in true information – the self-disclosure of God. Our hearts and minds (will and reason) must be illuminated by the Spirit of God through the Word of God. "So faith comes from hearing, and hearing through the word of Christ" (Romans 10:17); "For God, who said, 'Let light shine out of darkness,' has shone in our hearts to give the light of the knowledge of the glory of God in the face of Jesus Christ" (2 Corinthians 4:6).

This surrendered trust also requires a release of my own attempts at redemption – attempts to appease the divine or show myself righteous before others. God says, "I will do this." I must entrust myself to him, confident that he will fulfill his promise. If I, however, continue to count on my own good deeds to attain divine acceptance, I am destined for the wrath of God. God's righteousness cannot be humanly achieved. My own goodness is an inadequate object of trust. I need the righteousness that must be credited through surrendered trust in the God who alone is worthy of such trust.

God said, "in Christ God was reconciling the world to himself, not counting their trespasses against them" (2 Corinthians 5:19). Do I trust his promise, or do I still feel that I need to earn God's favor? When I entrust myself to him, I rest confidently in the *propitiatory* and *redemptive* work of Jesus Christ: he absorbed the wrath of God in my place, rescued me from the domain of darkness, and released me to a loving relationship with God. My surrendered trust credits his righteousness to me. Since my fundamental problem is the unrighteousness of self-preeminence, I must surrender my autocracy – the belief that I am the greatest and most important reality – and any attempt at self-righteousness. I must recognize that I am utterly at the mercy of an infinite, holy, sovereign God. Jesus made this unmistakably clear when he told his followers, "unless your righteousness exceeds that of the scribes and Pharisees, you will never enter the kingdom of heaven" (Matthew 5:20). His assertion must have shocked the people of his day because the scribes and Pharisees were

> **My surrendered trust credits his righteousness to me.**

> **I must have an accurate understanding of God as *he has disclosed himself.***

considered the epitome of righteousness. The righteousness required for God's kingdom is a righteousness that matches God's holiness, which can only come from God. This righteousness requires my surrender and my confession that I cannot redeem myself.

I must have an accurate understanding of God *as he has disclosed himself.* God has revealed himself clearly in person, in word, and in history: "And this is eternal life, that they know you, the only true God, and Jesus Christ whom you have sent" (John 17:3). If my knowledge of God is distorted, then my trust is inaccurate. I am trusting something other than the self-disclosed Creator. My faith is in the god of my own imagination, creation, passion, or even tradition. An inaccurate object of trust cannot save me from the wrath my unrighteousness deserves. Adam and Eve trusted in their distorted perception of God. Ultimately, their own passion and ambition led them to separation from God who alone could sustain and satisfy them.

But now the foundation is laid, the work has been done, and my debt has been paid. God stands ready to credit me with his righteousness the moment I surrender and entrust myself in faith to Jesus Christ:

> "You are the greatest and most important reality. I am not. I am fallen and sinful from the rebellion that has taken me from you, like a branch broken from the tree. From you I have fallen, to you I must return.

Your Son came to take my judgment, the wrath required by your holiness, to rescue me from slavery and to liberate me to you.

Therefore, I surrender to you, my creator and redeemer, and entrust myself to what Jesus has done to make me acceptable to you."

Upon this surrender, Christ's righteousness becomes ours! Our surrendered faith opens the floodgate to God's "grace upon grace" (John 1:16), and the righteousness of the perfect Son of God flows into our being. This exchange is the key scriptural doctrine of imputation. "For our sake he made him to be sin who knew no sin, so that in him we might become the righteousness of God" (2 Corinthians 5:21). Righteousness *is* attainable, — not by my merit or efforts of righteousness, but through imputation of Christ's righteousness by faith alone.

> **Righteousness *is* attainable, — not by my merit or efforts of righteousness, but through imputation of Christ's righteousness by faith alone.**

Righteousness will be counted to us who believe in him who raised from the dead Jesus our Lord, who was delivered up for our trespasses and raised for our justification (Romans 4:24-25).

I can now stand confidently before God, on this foundation alone:

> And be found in him, not having a righteousness of my own that comes from the law, but that which comes through faith in Christ, the righteousness from God that depends on faith (Philippians 3:9).

Think About It

1. Can you give examples of how we feel we need to redeem ourselves?

2. Why is it counter intuitive that we must receive the righteousness we cannot achieve?

3. People commonly talk in terms of *how much* faith they or others may have. How does the doctrine of imputation change the equation?

4. How is faith more than mere positive thinking?

CHAPTER 5

The Declaration: **Justification**

You are who God says you are.

For all have sinned and fall short of the glory
of God, and are justified by his grace as a gift,
through the redemption that is in Christ Jesus.
Romans 3:23-24

In a thousand ways society tells you every day that you
are worthless because you have no achievement.[11]
Miroslav Volf

God created us to know and enjoy him, but for this to happen, he must have a good reason to justify us – unrighteous beings held hostage by our own rebellion. Understanding the gospel is understanding that we are unjust beings.

> **Understanding the gospel is understanding that we are unjust beings.**

---

[11] Miroslav Volf, *Against the Tide: Love in a Time of Petty Dreams and Persisting Enmities,* (Wm. B. Eerdmans Publishing Co., 2010) p.137

We must acknowledge that there is evil within us, and that evil cannot coexist with God. He will forbear it for a time (see Romans 3:25), but because his essence is perfectly good, he must deal with sin. If he is good, he will necessarily oppose evil and ultimately destroy it. The dilemma arises when we acknowledge that evil exists *in* us. Through Jesus Christ's propitiation – sacrificing his perfect life – God dealt with sin by Christ taking the crushing weight of God's wrath. Christ paid the price for our redemption. Remember, we have been bought back *from* the captivity of our own rebellion, liberated *to* life in Christ.

Perspective

From a human perspective, this is history. But God's perspective is infinite and transcendent; he knows perfectly, absolutely, and concurrently all that is or could be known. He has known those who are his own from eternity, but we are confined to exist in time and space. We are born bearing God's image, we grow, and we encounter his revelation. Through faith I can entrust myself to Jesus Christ who is the propitiation for my sins, the one who has purchased my redemption. Only then is his righteousness credited to me. Now that I have his righteousness by faith, I am

> Now that I have his righteousness by faith, I am *justified* before a holy God.

justified before a holy God. *Justification* implies that justice has been served: God's wrath has been satisfied and Christ's righteousness has been credited. The significance of justification then, is that I am made right and declared righteous. Paul affirms the truth of Christ's work in history, and our surrender in time and space, set against God's transcendent perspective and purpose; "And those whom he predestined he also called, and those whom he called he also justified, and those whom he justified he also glorified" (Romans 8:29).

I will either enjoy God forever or I will not. There are no other options. If I am to enjoy God forever, he must have a basis upon which I (an unrighteous rebel) can be in his holy presence. This introduces us to the unique position of Christ as the "mediator between God and men" (I Timothy 2:5). When I surrender myself in faith to Christ, *then* his righteousness is credited to me, and *then* I become justified before God. The basis of this justification is propitiation and redemption through Jesus. Christ is mediator, in that as the God-man absorbed the judgment of God on the cross, he represented mankind. My lack of righteousness, my evil, and my sinfulness put Christ on the cross to experience the wrath of God – for me. He acted in my place. But as mediator between God and man, he also represented God *to* man, conveying God's pardoning grace. Not only was it my sin that put Jesus on the cross, but it was also God's holiness, justice, love, and mercy. God's grace put Jesus there.

Understanding Forgiveness

We commonly struggle to forgive someone who has hurt us, often because we misunderstand what it means to forgive. Too often, we believe that to forgive means we just have to forget the wrongdoing and move on with life as if to say, "I'm just going to pretend it never happened." Our human idea of forgiveness amounts to the proverbial "sweeping under the rug" of dropped food. Eventually, the food cannot be forgotten because of the smell. This is not true forgiveness. If God forgave a single sin by just closing his eyes as if to say, "Oh, that's okay, I'll overlook it," he would no longer be moral, just, or righteous. God cannot ignore *any* sin because he is absolutely holy – he is perfect. Every sin must be punished. This brings out the striking statement that John made: "He is the propitiation for our sins, and not for ours only but also for the sins of the whole world" (1 John 2:2). What sins did Christ cover when he absorbed the blow of God's wrath? He paid the price for every sin — past, present, and future.

> **Forgiveness is offered because every sin has been punished.**

What an astounding thought! This truth was echoed by Paul when he asserted, "in Christ God was reconciling the world to himself, not counting their trespasses against them" (2 Corinthians 5:19). Let us be careful to see this accurately. "Not counting their trespasses against them" is *not* the same thing as crediting righteousness to them. Forgiveness is offered because every sin has been punished. That is what Christ experienced on the cross. Does that create any wonder in your thinking, that God would do this?

The Necessary Foundation

As Jesus walked the road to Emmaus with two disciples after his resurrection, he used the word *necessary*. "'Was it not necessary that the Christ should suffer these things and enter into his glory?'" (Luke 24:26). *Necessary* means it had to happen – it was inevitable, or nothing else matters. The writer of Hebrews used the term *fitting*. "For it was fitting that he, for whom and by whom all things exist, in bringing many sons to glory, should make the founder of their salvation perfect through suffering" (Hebrews 2:10). Christ is our mediator— representing man by absorbing God's holy, necessary judgment, and representing God by conveying mercy, love, and a readiness to forgive. God's righteousness is vindicated, and the believing sinner is justified. The foundation is the historical reality of the propitiation of Christ and the redemption price he paid – that is history. When I, as one created in God's image by him and for him, respond to God's self-disclosure by trusting what God has revealed and place my faith

> God's righteousness is vindicated, and the believing sinner is justified.

in Christ's propitiatory, redemptive work, then his righteousness is imputed (credited) to me. I am then justified before God.

Meeting the Requirements

Before going any further, let me address an apparent contradiction in two texts of Scripture – both in the words of Paul. Romans 2:13, "For it is not the hearers of the law who are righteous before God, but the doers of the law who will be justified," appears to contradict Romans 3:20, "For by works of the law no human being will be justified in his sight." So, which is it – "the doers of the law will be justified," or "by works of the law no human being will be justified"? The point of these texts is that only those who maintain the law to perfection will be justified. Interestingly, Paul, before his conversion to faith in Christ, believed he was "as to righteousness under the law, blameless" (Philippians 3:6). The law was God's righteous requirement. If I keep the law perfectly, can I then be accepted before God? Isn't that what Romans 2:13 says, "the doers of the law will be justified"? In this text, Scripture speaks of our incapacity, which the law made abundantly clear. No mere man can perfectly meet the righteous requirement of God's law. That is why we

> No mere man can perfectly meet the righteous requirement of God's law. That is why we need Christ.

need Christ. He represented God to man, and he represented man before God. When we think of the work of Christ, our minds immediately recall his death, burial, and resurrection; but we also need to consider the life Christ lived before his passion. Jesus lived a perfect life, and it was because of his perfection that his death on the cross counted for us. His perfect life sacrificed paid for our redemption. As Jesus took on the wrath of his holy Father and experienced relational separation from God, he said "I thirst," (John 19:28). I believe it is possible that he was not just physically thirsty, but also felt the deep spiritual craving of a parched soul abandoned by the source of life – the ultimate meaning of *death*. The death of Christ was not just exemplary — it was substitutionary.

Romans 4:24 tells us that the righteousness of Christ is imputed to us who believe: "It will be counted to us who believe in him." (The word "it" in this verse refers to Christ's righteousness in verses 13-23). Romans 3 speaks of this justification: "For all have sinned and fall short of the glory of God, and are justified by his grace as a gift, through the redemption that is in Christ Jesus, whom God put forward as a propitiation by his blood, to be received by faith" (Romans 3:23-25). For the believer in Jesus, the righteousness of God is not *achieved*, it is *received* through faith. Nor is the act of divine justification an arbitrary decision that God made. It is solidly founded on the propitiatory, redemptive work of Jesus Christ. I entrust myself in faith to this Redeemer, and his righteousness is credited to me. The righteousness of the perfect Son of God flows into me. Not only are the floodgates of God's righteousness opened, but the gates of God's wrath on me are permanently sealed. This is the basis of my justification.

> There is therefore now no condemnation for those who are in Christ Jesus. For the law of the Spirit of life has set you free in Christ Jesus from the law of sin and death. For God has done what the law, weakened by the flesh, could not do. By sending his own Son in the likeness of sinful flesh and for sin, he condemned sin in the flesh, in order that the righteous requirement of the law might be fulfilled in us, who walk not according to the flesh but according to the Spirit (Romans 8:1-4).

The Declaration

God justified me; I did not and cannot justify myself. Justification is a divine declaration, which makes it a permanent state for the believer. Paul stated in Ephesians 2:6 that God has "seated us with him in the heavenly places in Christ Jesus." The justified believer is seated – it is an

The justified believer is seated – it is an established position.

established position. I (once a rebel sinner, unrighteous by nature) am accepted into the presence of God who is infinitely holy, infinitely righteous, and infinitely good. Paul stated this another way when he said, "Your life is hidden with Christ in God" (Colossians 3:3). Again, God's declaration of justifying the believing sinner is not a random decision; Christ is the basis for justification.

I have heard God described as a military tank. When I deny or oppose God, I am like a person going up to a military tank in opposition and kicking it. The tank does not get hurt; I do. The only way to be rescued from the wrath of holy God is found in the protection of God himself. The cross is Christ reaching down, pulling me up into the tank to protect me from God's consuming wrath. I am safely in the tank, I am with God, and I am justified. Having surrendered in faith to Christ, I am safely enveloped in the perfect righteousness of Christ.

God's justification of the believer is also more than just acquittal or being forgiven. Justification is a judicial declaration of God, as when the judge in a courtroom makes a ruling by hitting his gavel on the bench. God declares me righteous! I am now in a condition acceptable to God. Christ absorbed the debt that was mine. Justification is Christ's righteousness in me.

> What I must remember is that God has credited to me the righteousness of Christ, and I therefore stand before him justified.

By this righteousness, I can truly follow Christ and be conformed to his image. When his righteousness is credited to me, I am not just a forgiven sinner; I am a righteous being – declared to be so by God himself.

This is how God sees the believing sinner. This concept may be a struggle to accept, which is why we must understand the distinction between justification and sanctification. Viewing myself as a righteous person is inconsistent with what I know of myself because I still have imperfections. *Justification* is the singular pronouncement in which God declares me righteous and accepts me, because Christ's righteousness has been credited to me. *Sanctification* is the lifelong process by which God continuously brings out that righteousness within me. But now he *has* something to bring out – the righteousness of Christ.

Our adversary the devil and his forces of darkness want me to forget this vital truth of justification. Satan's ambition as "the accuser" (Revelation 12:10) is to distract me with my imperfections and failings. What I must remember is that God has credited to me the righteousness of Christ, and I therefore stand before him justified. I am accepted before God, and *nothing* changes that. What God has revealed about me in his self-disclosure must be held true over how I may feel in any given moment of weakness. Even in my failings, God looks at me and sees Christ because I – the believing sinner – am *in Christ*. J.C. Ryle said:

Without justification it is impossible to have real peace. Conscience forbids it. Sin is a mountain between a man and God and must be taken away. The sense of guilt lies heavy on the heart and must be removed. Unpardoned sin will murder peace. The true Christian knows all this well. His peace arises from a consciousness of his sins being forgiven, and his guilt being put away. He has peace with God, because he is justified.[12]

From the moment of surrendered trust – I am accepted by God in Christ. God does not accept me by probation. He does not say, "You are accepted if you do this, and if you do that." My justification before God in Christ is in no way based upon my own performance. That would be regress into the false theology of human merit. Rather, my position in Christ is sealed — it is secure. That ought to bring great comfort, encourage-ment, and peace – because nothing can change my posi-tion before God. I do not have to keep working hard

> The key truth about the doctrine of justification is this: there is nothing we can do to make God accept and love us more. There is nothing we can do to make God accept and love us less.

[12] J.C. Ryle in Foundations of Faith. *Christianity Today*, Vol. 35, no. 8.

for his ongoing acceptance. This key truth of the gospel distinguishes the God of the Bible from all others. The gods of human imagination require the individual's performance to achieve divine favor, but God's grace grants righteousness to be received by faith – front-loaded justification.

God's forgiveness does not set me free to do anything I desire. That is misunderstanding and abusing the gospel of grace. But in Christ, I have an unchanging position of acceptance before God. He is working in me to manifest Christ's righteousness externally, while the foundational truth of justification – that I am accepted in him – remains steadfast. "Who shall bring any charge against God's elect? It is God who justifies" (Romans 8:33). I will not live a perfect life, I still must battle the sinful flesh, but nothing changes the fact that I am accepted in Christ before God. When we think, "I need to do this or that or God is not going to be happy with me," our thinking is inconsistent with God's grace. The key truth about the doctrine of justification is this: there is nothing we can do to make God accept and love us more. There is nothing we can do to make God accept and love us less. We are accepted before God *in* Christ.

God is in the business of shaping our lives to bring out the righteousness of Christ. He is in the process of molding and conforming us into the image of Jesus, so that our lives point people to God and his goodness. For that reason, Paul said, "work out your own salvation with fear and trembling, for it is God who works in you, both to will and to work for his good pleasure" (Philippians 2:12–13). In other words, nurture and bring to outward expression that divine life within. Let the righteousness of Christ mold your affections and attitudes, transform your thoughts and desires, and manifest in your daily walk. We will cover this later in greater detail, but for now, contemplate the comforting and compelling truth of Romans 5:1-2: "Therefore, since we have been justified by faith, we have peace with God through our Lord Jesus Christ. Through him we have also obtained access by faith into this grace in which we stand, and we rejoice in hope of the glory of God."

Think About It

1. How is God justified to justify the believing sinner?

2. What is the chief difference between *justification* and *sanctification*?

3. What is encouraging to the believer about this contrast?

4. What makes the doctrine of justification unique among faith systems?

CHAPTER 6

The Outcome: **Reconciliation**

Return to the One for whom you were designed.

We also rejoice in God through our Lord Jesus Christ,
through whom we have now received reconciliation.

Romans 5:11

They will see his face, and his name
will be on their foreheads.

Revelation 22:4

There is coming a day when every human being will stand before God and give account of his life. No matter how righteous our life was, we will all fall short of the righteousness, beauty, and perfection of God – unless we lived in *his* righteousness. We need righteousness, and God now has made that righteousness available. We have no basis of boasting because of the doctrine of imputation – righteousness is credited to us through faith, based on his propitiation and his redemption on the cross. Then we are justified, declared acceptable before a righteous, holy God. Now that we are accepted before God, we are *reconciled* to him.

Access

"Therefore, since we have been justified by faith, we have peace with God through our Lord Jesus Christ. Through him we have also obtained access by faith into this grace in which we stand, and we rejoice in hope of the glory of God" (Romans 5:1-2). Once, we fell short of the glory of God, we became enemies of God and alienated from him; now, in Christ, we rejoice in hope of the glory of God. The word *access* is a powerful term. We are given strong imagery of this access as Jesus was on the cross and the veil of the temple was torn (Mark 15:38, Luke 23:45). The place of God's presence – where he said he would meet with us – is now accessible to us.

The place of God's presence – where he said he would meet with us – is now accessible to us.

So, the author of Hebrews wrote, "Let us then with confidence draw near to the throne of grace, that we may receive mercy and find grace to help in time of need" (Hebrews 4:16).

God, in all his holiness, the perfect Sovereign, sits in his throne room – a throne room to which I now have access. I am welcomed in because I am accepted before holy God. I am reconciled to him. This is a foundational truth of the gospel. Ray Ortlund writes:

[Jesus] builds his new kind of community with sinners so bad they can't give God a single reason why he should even notice them. He gathers into his arms those very sinners and says to them, *Congratulations! You stand to inherit everything worth having forever![13]*

Unearned Acceptance

In 2006, Warren Buffett, the world's second richest man at the time, announced that he would donate 85 percent of his fortune (approximately 37.5 billion dollars) to charitable foundations. Commenting on his generosity, Buffett said, "There's more than one way to get to heaven, but this is a great way."[14] Before we judge him too harshly, we must confess that his statement demonstrates a natural way to think – I have performed something that deserves an audience before the Creator. The doctrine of reconciliation reminds us that it is God who reconciles us to himself. There is nothing in ourselves or in our efforts that earns his acceptance and favor. There is nothing that I can do to reconcile myself to God. The point of this illustration is that the object of trust for my eternal state is what matters. The sacrificed blood of Jesus has washed away the penalty of

---

[13] Ray Ortlund, in the forward to Tony Merida's book *Loving Your Church*, (The Good Book Company, 2021), p.11-12

[14] https://www.nbcnews.com/id/wbna13541144

sin; the righteousness of Christ is credited to those who, once enemies, believe and are now seated at his table.

Many people reject the gospel because they are not willing to accept that they are alienated from God and are his enemy. God's abhorrence of sin does not make him the enemy of sinners, nor does he seek their ill. As was discussed in chapter two, man declared war on God by walking away from him. This war started in the garden of Eden when our first parents were tempted to believe that there was something that would bring them greater satisfaction than God. They chose to abandon God, to cross over his loving boundaries, and seek their satisfaction and security apart from him. Man rebelled and became acquainted with good *and evil*.

Rebels

The consequence of man walking away from God was this: "The wrath of God is revealed from heaven against all ungodliness and unrighteousness of men, who by their unrighteousness suppress the truth" (Romans 1:18). God must oppose evil because he is perfectly good and holy. So, "since they did not see fit to acknowledge God, God gave them up to a debased mind to do what ought not to be done" (Romans 1:28). That

When we consider that the Sovereign over creation marveled at their unbelief, we can clearly see the deep, dark deception of the human heart.

is the foundational dilemma of unrighteous humanity. We do not want him because we think we know better than he does. Even Christ was astonished at that level of pride and self-delusion. He came to bring reconciliation by showing the Father. He lived perfectly and performed miracles. Yet while Jesus walked and worked among men, Mark tells us, "he marveled because of their unbelief" (Mark 6:6). When we consider that the Sovereign over creation marveled at their unbelief, we can clearly see the deep, dark deception of the human heart. This unbelief did not take Jesus by surprise. Jesus knew and expected their unbelief because God had known it from eternity. But he still marveled to see the depths of human pride and self-preeminence that led the religious leaders to ignore the truth – even as he walked among them and fulfilled the prophecies that they studied. All this powerful, glorious information was available to them visually, audibly, and experientially, yet people said, "I don't want it! It will only get in the way of my precious agenda and pleasures." Jesus marveled at this darkness of the human heart. This darkness is why we need to be reconciled to God. Paul wrote, "and you, who once were alienated and hostile in mind, doing evil deeds" (Colossians 1:21). My enmity with God begins in my mind with my desire to suppress him and my attitude that I know better than he does. Therefore, I will seek after other objects of satisfaction and security. Yet, "he has now reconciled in his body of flesh by his death, in order to present you holy and blameless and above reproach before him" (Colossians 1:22). What a colossal act of mercy and grace!

Reconciled Rebels

Several years ago, a man by the name of Jesse Jacobs created an apology hotline. People unable or unwilling to unburden their conscience in person called the hotline to leave an apology message on an answering machine. Each week, thirty to fifty calls were logged as people apologized for things from adultery to embezzlement. This hotline did not provide these individuals with forgiveness or righteousness, but it did reveal something else. Jacobs said of his hotline:

> The hotline offers participants a chance to alleviate their guilt and to some degree, to own up to their misdeeds. I'm just hoping that these people will feel better themselves just by getting what's been bothering them off their chest. One caller of the hotline remarked, "I hope this apology will cleanse me and basically purify my soul. God knows I need it."[15]

Each of us instinctively recognizes that we are flawed. We mess up and know that we need forgiveness

---

[15] Samantha Gross, "Hot Line Offers 'Sorry' Service," *www. WashingtonTimes.com* (5-31-04)

and reconciliation. These are not possible without righteousness. Christ has come to provide righteousness for us to bring us back to God: "For Christ also suffered once for sins, the righteous for the unrighteous, that he might bring us to God" (1 Peter 3:18).

That basic longing, that thirst for forgiveness and reconciliation, exists in every human heart because we have fallen short of the glory of God. God, in Christ, has made that reconciliation possible.

The Greek word for *reconcile* is *katallasso*, often used as a financial term. For example, if I gave you a dollar to exchange for some coins, you owe me a dollar, but you give me three quarters. That twenty-five cents would still need to be reconciled. The word *reconciliation* has the very real sense of taking something that has fallen short and making it right. Paul wrote, "while we were enemies we were reconciled to God by the death of his Son" (Romans 5:10). Reconciliation happened *to* us; we do not and cannot reconcile ourselves to God. Also, God does not need reconciliation, because he is unchanging. Rather, we have rebelled against him in attitude, intent, and behavior, thinking we can do life better — only to be held in bondage to our passions and the resulting power and penalty of sin. We have crossed over his loving boundaries. We need to be reconciled

> **The word *reconciliation* has the very real sense of taking something that has fallen short and making it right.**

to God, and he has made that possible. God is in the business of reconciling mankind to himself.

When Paul wrote, "we were reconciled to God by the death of his Son," he takes us back to the foundation of Christ's propitiatory and redemptive work. This is the basis on which God can reconcile us. God is righteous and holy. He *must* deal with sin. The importance of this doctrine is sadly falling out of standing in many churches today. One of the great songs of modern hymnody states, "And on the cross as Jesus died / The wrath of God was satisfied."[16] That song lyric celebrates the doctrine of propitiation. There are some churches that have changed that line to read, "And on the cross as Jesus died / The love of God was magnified." Eliminating the doctrine of propitiation presented so clearly in Scripture relegates the death of Christ to being nothing more than a good example. But the wrath of God needed to be satisfied. Propitiation is necessary or we would be utterly without hope, destined for the necessary wrath of a holy God. Without propitiation, redemption, and the imputation of righteousness through faith in Christ, God could not reconcile us to

> **Without propitiation, redemption, and the imputation of righteousness through faith in Christ, God could not reconcile us to himself.**

---

[16] *In Christ Alone,* by Keith Getty & Stuart Townend, Copyright © 2001 Thankyou Music

himself. Christ's substitutionary death is foundational to our reconciliation to God.

Divine Initiative

Our reconciliation is a wonderful and marvelous thing, but there is more! Paul continues in Romans 5:10, "much more, now that we are reconciled, shall we be saved by his life." The words "much more" imply initiation by God. The redemption of mankind is not man moving towards God or man coming back to God. Redemption is God moving towards man in order to reconcile man to himself. That is why he sent his Son to pay the debt that we owe. When I was alienated from God, he was my judge: "Whoever has the Son has life; whoever does not have the Son of God does not have life" (1 John 5:12). "Whoever believes in him is not condemned, but whoever does not believe is condemned already, because he has not believed in the name of the only Son of God" (John 3:18). When I am not in Christ, I do not have the righteousness of Christ credited to me, which means I am still under the judgment of God. But when I am in Christ, I am then imputed with his righteousness. I am justified before God and reconciled to him. That means he is no longer my judge – he is my father, and a father interacts with his children with love and care.

Relationship

When Paul wrote, "we shall be saved by his life," he affirmed the triumph of the resurrection of Christ. Now God has lavished me with the riches of his grace. Jesus did *not* just die to pay my debt; now I have moved from death to life – I am alive – a new creation in relationship with God. Reconciliation is also a relational term. Now that I am reconciled to God, I can interact and commune with him. This relationship is the very design and intent of my existence. Jesus said, "Because I live, you also will live" (John 14:19), and "this is eternal life, that they know you, the only true God, and Jesus Christ whom you have sent" (John 17:3). We are mistaken when we make our faith system about "bad" people becoming "good" because that is what merit-based religions are about. Rather, God in Christ brings dead people to life. There is a progression of salvation; at the point in history when I entrusted myself to Jesus Christ, he imputed his righteousness to me, he justified me, then he reconciled me. Now I am on the path of sanctification *by walking with God*. God is molding me on the inside, conforming me to the image of his Son, and eventually I

> Now that I am reconciled to God, I can interact and commune with him.

> Man's rebellion against God was like a branch wishing to be free from the tree.

85

will experience glorification where I am forever with him, perfectly like him (see Romans 8:29-30).

The night of his betrayal, Jesus gave his disciples a strong and vivid illustration of the power of reconciliation: "I am the vine; you are the branches. Whoever abides in me and I in him, he it is that bears much fruit, for apart from me you can do nothing" (John 15:5). Man's rebellion against God was like a branch wishing to be free from the tree. The sinful branch irrationally wished its own demise by removing itself from the tree. A branch severed from the tree can do nothing *but* die. The branch must be grafted back into the tree if it is to live. Only in Christ, who reconciles us to the Creator and Source of life, can we have life. The branch that is vitally connected to the vine (or tree) draws life from its source – life that is productive. The branch does not need to exert effort in trying to produce fruit; the fruit production is an outflow of the branch abiding in the vine. God's purpose and model for my life is the life of his Son, Jesus. It is through the pursuit and development of our relationship with him that we become like him – a pursuit that is possible only because we have been reconciled to him. This is the ultimate purpose of our

> It is through the pursuit and development of our relationship with him that we become like him – a pursuit that is possible only because we have been reconciled to him.

reconciliation to God through the gospel of grace in Jesus Christ.

Paul expanded on this when he wrote, "More than that, we also rejoice in God through our Lord Jesus Christ, through whom we have now received reconciliation" (Romans 5:11). The Greek word translated into English as *rejoice* means to glory, boast, or promote. When I rejoice about something, I champion and thereby promote it. God reconciles us to himself with the intent that we will glory in and promote our reconciliation. His chief instruments of reconciliation are those whom he has reconciled already. Just as a liberated POW wants to communicate the greatness of the liberator and the joys of liberty to those yet captive, we communicate the greatness of our liberator and the joys of our liberty in Christ to those not yet reconciled.

Captivated

It is possible, sadly, to be in Christ yet still perceive God as our judge who stands ready to condemn us every time we step out of line. If that is our perception of God, then that is how we will represent him to others. If our representation of the walk of faith is more about morality, then our perception of God is probably not of the one who has done all the work

If our religion is one of criticism and judgment, then we hold the false idea that the "bad" must become "good."

necessary to reconcile us to himself. People cannot just "get in line" with our Christian ideas of morality. God is the one that must reconcile them, and only if they have been credited with the righteousness of Christ. If our religion is one of criticism and judgment, then we hold the false idea that the "bad" must become "good." God has given us "the ministry of reconciliation" (Romans 5:11), not a ministry of moral demands and judgment. The wrath of God is necessary, but he has saved us from that wrath. He has entrusted the ministry of reconciliation to those already reconciled. Paul made this abundantly clear:

> All this is from God, who through Christ reconciled us to himself and gave us the ministry of reconciliation; that is, in Christ God was reconciling the world to himself, not counting their trespasses against them, and entrusting to us the message of reconciliation. Therefore, we are ambassadors for Christ, God making his appeal through us. We implore you on behalf of Christ, be reconciled to God (2 Corinthians 5:18-20).

That is a powerful purpose for our interaction with people in our world – friends, relatives, associates, and neighbors. We who are reconciled serve as agents of

We who are reconciled serve as agents of reconciliation.

reconciliation. Many are fighting a lonely battle against God. Let us be the ones who communicate that God has opened the gates of reconciliation and peace.

You may be familiar with the story of Nate Saint, who was one of five missionaries to Ecuador in the 1950s. While trying to make contact with the Waodani people, the five men were murdered by the very people they were trying to reach. In a testament to forgiveness, the families of the slain missionaries later returned to the tribe, eventually winning many of them to Christ. Nate Saint's son, Steve, was asked if there was a specific moment of reconciliation between the families of the deceased missionaries and the Waodani tribe. This is how he answered:

> It was a developing thing, but I think the point of reconciliation really was with Mincaye, (the man who killed his father) and my Aunt Rachel. Mincaye said to Aunt Rachel (Nate's sister), "You said that the Creator is very strong."

> Aunt Rachel said, "Mincaye, He is very strong. He made everything here, even the dirt."

> Mincaye said, "You said that He could clean somebody's heart. My heart being very, very dark, can He clean even my heart?"

And Aunt Rachel said, "Being very strong, He can clean even your heart."

In her journal she wrote that Mincaye got up and walked away but that the next morning he came back excited. He said, "What you said is true. Speaking to God has cleaned my heart. Now it's clear like the sky when it has no clouds in it".

That was the real beginning of reconciliation.[17]

This is a beautiful example of God's reconciliation. When we understand that God is a reconciling God, we can see the powerful possibilities that exist for healing in human relationships. When we are reconciled to God, in relationship with him, our mission is to bring people to reconciliation with God. It is not about making "bad" people "good." It is, rather, about introducing people to the God who reconciles, bringing them from death to life.

> When we understand that God is a reconciling God, we can see the powerful possibilities that exist for healing in human relationships.

---

[17] Amanda Knoke, *Decision* (January 2006), p. 20

Think About It

1. What does it mean to be an enemy of God?

2. Give an example of a reconciled relationship you have experienced.

3. What does it mean to draw life from the tree as a reconciled branch?

4. How does your reconciliation to God impact your relationships?

CHAPTER 7

The Change: **Regeneration**

Radical transformation and realized purpose.

We were buried therefore with him by baptism
into death, in order that, just as Christ was
raised from the dead by the glory of the Father,
we too might walk in newness of life.

Romans 6:4

God creates out of nothing. *Wonderful*, you say.
Yes, to be sure, but He does what is still more
wonderful: He makes saints out of sinners.

Soren Kierkegaard

*P*eople don't change – they say.
There is a higher authority
in the gospel of grace. God's
business is life transformation
– changing people into reflec-
tions of Jesus Christ so that
others can empirically recognize

**People don't
change – they
say. There is a
higher authority
in the gospel
of grace.**

the goodness of God. His goodness leads people to repentance.

My first encounter with genuine life transformation was while I spent the first twelve years of life in Colombia as the son of church-planting missionaries. My dad encountered Marcelino, a man who worked long, back-breaking hours at a tire shop. On payday, Marcelino's first stop was the bar, searching for escape from the meaningless hardships of life. His pent-up frustrations mixed with alcohol would result in his beaten wife and children cowering before their angry dad. But Marcelino heard the gospel faithfully communicated and surrendered in faith to Christ. Through many months of discipleship, as a deer thirsting for water, he lapped up the life-changing truths of the gospel of grace, and his life and family were radically transformed. Years later, when our family departed from Colombia, Marcelino was entrusted with the task of pastoring the church. God's work is transforming lives.

Because we were created and designed to know God and enjoy him, he is the point to our existence. Without righteousness, however, not only can we not know and enjoy him, but we will be doomed to an eternity without him. When I entrust myself in faith to Jesus Christ, his righteousness becomes mine. Having that righteousness leads to my justification because God declares me righteous. I am now reconciled back to God — to know him, to enjoy him, and to walk with him.

The Branch Reconciled to Its Life Source

God's mission is reconciliation that results in life transformation. This change is made
possible based only on the objective truths of what Christ accom-
plished in history – his perfect life, his death, his burial,
and his resurrection. When I entrust myself in faith
to Jesus Christ, I am not *just* a forgiven sinner – I am
a *new creation*. The objective truths I believed in faith
(my surrendered trust) become subjective realities in my
believing heart. My attitudes and affections are transformed and aligned with God's. The New Testament
writers affirmed this constantly in their writings.
Consider, for example, the contrast that Paul made
between unregenerate and regenerate life:

> **God's mission
> is reconciliation
> that results in life
> transformation.**

> For we ourselves were once foolish, disobe-
> dient, led astray, slaves to various passions
> and pleasures, passing our days in malice
> and envy, hated by others and hating one
> another. But when the goodness and loving
> kindness of God our Savior appeared, he
> saved us, not because of works done by us
> in righteousness, but according to his own
> mercy, by the washing of *regeneration and
> renewal of the Holy Spirit*, whom he poured
> out on us richly through Jesus Christ our

Savior, so that being justified by his grace we might become heirs according to the hope of eternal life (Titus 3:3-7 *emphasis added*).

Salvation is not a matter of a person choosing to clean up his life. Instead, regeneration launches a transformation in the believer's life. Paul described those who are not in Christ as alienated from God; they are "dead in the trespasses and sins in which you once walked" (Ephesians 2:1-2). They are separated from God. When I was dead in sin, I was a branch severed from the tree lying on the ground. "Dead" is the only way to describe it. The only thing that branch could do is die. It could not pick itself up and reconcile itself back into the tree. God alone reconciles. He raises up the branch and grafts it back into the tree – the source of life. Now that branch draws life from the tree – it is regenerated. Christ's life is now flowing through me, the believer. David Needham expresses it well: "At the heart of my humanness – spirit – there is life where there was never life before."[18] Jesus Christ transforms me from the inside, where the problem lies, and then replaces the old with the new. This is the beautiful doctrine of regeneration.

> God alone reconciles. He raises up the branch and grafts it back into the tree – the source of life.

---

[18] David Needham, *Birthright,* (Multnomah Publishers, 1999) p.62

The Seed

While the exact word *regeneration* was not used in Paul's letter to the Roman church, the teaching was abundantly clear as the apostle taught the foundational truths of the gospel of grace. Paul first pointed out the unrighteousness of humanity, then the available *righteousness* of Christ based on his *propitiation* and the price paid for our *redemption*. That righteousness is credited to those of us who believe (*imputation*), thereby we are *justified* – declared acceptable before holy God – and we are *reconciled* to God. Woven through this progression of concepts is the doctrine of *regeneration*, whereby God makes the sinner a new creation in Christ. Look how Paul described this newness:

> We were buried therefore with him by baptism into death, in order that, just as Christ was raised from the dead by the glory of the Father, *we too might walk in newness of life.* For if we have been united with him in a death like his, we shall certainly be united with him in a resurrection like his. We know that *our old self was crucified with him* in order that the body of sin might be brought to nothing, so that we would *no longer be enslaved to sin*. For one who has died has been *set free from sin*. Now if we have died with Christ, we believe that we will also

live with him. We know that Christ, being raised from the dead, will never die again; death no longer has dominion over him. For the death he died he died to sin, once for all, but the life he lives he lives to God. So you also must *consider yourselves dead to sin and alive to God in Christ Jesus.* Let not sin therefore reign in your mortal body, to make you obey its passions. Do not present your members to sin as instruments for unrighteousness, but present yourselves to God as those who have been brought from death to life, and your members to God as instruments for righteousness. For sin will have no dominion over you, since you are not under law but under grace (Romans 6:4-14 *emphasis added*).

Through faith (my surrendered trust), I am united with Christ in his death and resurrection. His history has now become mine, which is why God sees me *in Christ,* robed in his righteousness. My justification before God is a positional reality; my reconciliation to God is life-generating and life changing – transformation into the image of Christ. This is possible because we are "dead to sin and alive to God." The word *dead* does not mean it is no longer possible for me to sin, but it means I am no longer bound and enslaved to sin. I do *not* have to obey it.

Peter and John pictured this reality of our newness in Christ with the metaphor of the seed. Peter wrote to believers:

> Having purified your souls by your obedience to the truth for a sincere brotherly love, love one another earnestly from a pure heart, since you have been born again, not of perishable seed but of imperishable, through the living and abiding word of God (I Peter 1:22-23).

Peter used the term *spora*, an agricultural metaphor which represents a farmer's seed. When the seed is planted, it grows and produces. We use this metaphor when we speak of planting seeds of truth. Jesus used it in the parable about the farmer sowing seed that falls onto either fertile ground or rocky ground. Jesus also used this metaphor in speaking of a person's life; if the seed is going to grow and produce, first it must die (John 12:24).[19] John, however, used a different word – *sperma* – when he said the believer is "born of God" and "God's seed abides in him" (I John 3:9). This is the imputed righteousness

I must have a righteousness that matches his if I am to have communion with God. We all were designed for communion with God. That is the definition of human success.

---

[19] I equate that with the surrendered trust of faith

of Christ – the newness that is ours. Using the word *sperma*, John created a picture to describe the transmission of the righteous nature of God to the believer. This transmission is necessary for communion with God and for the process of being transformed into the image of Jesus Christ. I must have a righteousness that matches his if I am to have communion with God. We all were designed for communion with God. That is the definition of human success.

There is now new life in me. John said something rather striking about this new reality. In 1 John 3:9 he wrote, "No one born of God makes a practice of sinning, for God's seed abides in him; and he cannot keep on sinning, because he has been born of God." John used an absolute negative which implies a fundamental difference in the child of God which was generated by the nature of the parent. God generates life in the believer, creating a fundamental difference at the core of his being. The Bible contrasts the believer who is regenerate (alive to God because he is reconciled), and the unbeliever who is unregenerate (dead in sin and alienated from God). One commentator writes, "The point here is that the child partakes of the nature of his parent. Thus, the thought of a sinless parent, God, who begets a child who only sins a little is far from the

God generates life in the believer, creating a fundamental difference at the core of his being.

author's mind."[20] We cannot think about the doctrine of regeneration as being Christians who just sin less often than unbelievers. That is not the Biblical doctrine of regeneration to which God is calling us.

> I am writing these things to you so that you may not sin. But if anyone does sin, we have an advocate with the Father, Jesus Christ the righteous. He is the propitiation for our sins, and not for ours only but also for the sins of the whole world (1 John 2:1-2).

John emphasizes the inward newness of the child of God, "whose whole bent of life is away from sin."[21]

The New Covenant

> "He saved us, not because of works done by us in righteousness, but according to his own mercy, by the washing of regeneration and renewal of the Holy Spirit"

The Greek word used by Paul for *regeneration* in Titus 3:5 is *palingenesia*. This is a compound word made by combining the words rendered in English as

---

[20] Zane Hodges in *The Bible Knowledge Commentary*, New Testament Ed., John F. Walvoord and Roy B. Zuck, Editors (Wheaton, IL; Victor Books, 1983), pp. 894-895

[21] *Bible Knowledge Commentary, NT ed., p.895*

genesis and *anew*. Paul also said, "Therefore if anyone is in Christ, he is a new creation. The old has passed away; behold, the new has come" (2 Corinthians 5:17). The Greek word used for *new* in this verse, *kainos*, means a new class, or a new kind. It does not refer to something that was fixed up, repolished, or refurbished – it refers to something that is entirely new.

The subsequent Greek word *ktisis* means "creation." This new creation is not something that was God's "plan B." This newness was promised in the Old Testament. The Mosaic Law (the old covenant) was a temporary covenant to a specific people for a specific time. It was not designed to be a permanent solution to the human problem of unrighteousness. In the old covenant, God foreshadowed and promised the new covenant and the newness that God would create in his people.

One place we find this new covenant is in the book of Ezekiel, where this new covenant was promised specifically to the people of Israel. But, as Paul made clear, in Christ we are "heirs according to promise" (Galatians 3:29). So, this covenant benefits all who are in Christ:

> I will sprinkle clean water on you, and you
> shall be clean from all your uncleannesses,
> and from all your idols I will cleanse you.
> And I will give you a new heart, and a new
> spirit I will put within you. And I will
> remove the heart of stone from your flesh
> and give you a heart of flesh. And I will

> put my Spirit within you, and cause you to
> walk in my statutes and be careful to obey
> my rules (Ezekiel 36:25-27).

What the prophet described is the transforming grace of God in we who are his people. Consider what is promised – sprinkling of "clean water" and replacing the "heart of stone" with a "heart of flesh." This is what Paul referred to as "the washing of regeneration" (Titus 3:5), and what John affirmed as God's forgiveness that "cleanses us from all unrighteousness" (1 John 1:9). With the phrase "heart of flesh" (Ezekiel 36:26), Ezekiel spoke not of "the flesh" (describing the fallen nature of man) but of living tissue. What is the difference between stone and living tissue? A stone is cold, lifeless, and void of relationship; it does not absorb or respond. Conversely, a heart made of living nerve and tissue is sensory and responsive. God does not just promise to take out a heart that is stone-cold, calloused, and unresponsive. He also promises to replace it with a heart of flesh — a living, sensing, responsive heart. This newness that God creates is the seed of God — the *spora* of which Peter wrote, and the *sperma* that John talked about. This is the new creation of the believer, that "new self" to which the apostle Paul appealed (Ephesians 4:24; Colossians 3:10).

The Spirit of God is the one who regenerates.

The Spirit of God is the one who regenerates. God promises that when we come to faith in Christ, the Holy Spirit takes up residence in the believer. "I will put my Spirit within you" (Ezekiel 36:27). The Spirit is the one who empowers us and transforms us into genuine obedience to Christ. In that way, "we are his workmanship, created in Christ Jesus for good works, which God prepared beforehand, that we should walk in them" (Ephesians 2:10). God's purpose is to develop the character of Jesus Christ in me. Because I have Christ's righteousness, I should focus on pursuing and walking with God to nurture and bring to outward expression the divine life now within me. This process of life change is God's purpose in the new covenant. This newness was launched by Jesus in his perfect life, his death, and his resurrection. The night before his death on the cross, Jesus instituted a rite of remembrance for his followers to keep. When he took the cup of wine, Jesus said, "this cup that is poured out for you is the new covenant in my blood" (Luke 22:20). Jesus wanted us to remember this covenant; it follows that we should know and understand it.

Benefits of the New Covenant

There are three benefits of the new covenant for us. First, in Christ, there is full forgiveness of our sins, whereas only a covering for sin was offered under the Law. Second, there is newness. The stone-cold heart has been replaced with a living, sensing heart capable of relating to our Creator and Redeemer. The heart is a metaphor for the seat of thought and desire in the person bearing God's image. God is transforming us and grants us newness in our attitudes and affections. Third, there is the empowering presence of his Holy Spirit for we who are reconciled to God. God's purpose to transform my life is not about me cleaning up my act, it is about God's transforming life and power within me that will flow upward to love and adore him and outward to point people to him.

> God's purpose to transform my life is not about me cleaning up my act, it is about God's transforming life and power within me that will flow upward to love and adore him and outward to point people to him.

Outward Expression of the Divine Life Within

For this divine life to develop within me, I must grasp the fact that I am reconciled to God and understand what is now true about me. I was once alienated from God, but now I *can* walk with God. I can do what he designed me to do: commune with him, and delight in him. When I walk in communion with him, I am transformed. Now his Spirit bears witness with my new spirit (the new inner person is in harmony with God's Spirit) that I am a child of God (Romans 8:16) and a fellow heir with Christ (v.17), and my spirit cries out, "Abba! Father!" (v.15). This paragraph uses deeply personal and relational language. My reconciliation to God is radically life-altering, because now I can be in deep, personal relationship with my loving Father instead of being alienated from and under the condemnation of my righteous and holy Judge.

The apostle Peter wrote, "he has granted to us his precious and very great promises, so that through them you may become partakers of the divine nature, having escaped from the corruption that is in the world because of sinful desire" (2 Peter 1:4). I must be labor-intensive in walking with God and pursuing him. In that passionate pursuit, my new nature grows and transforms me in practical ways and outward expression (what people can see). My new inner self that is created in Christ Jesus is still housed in a corruptible tent. My flesh – my physical body – is habituated in sin. Paul informed the Galatian believers, "the desires of the flesh are against the Spirit, and the desires of the Spirit are against the flesh, for these are opposed to each other, to keep you from doing the things you want to do" (Galatians 5:17). Because of this, there is an ongoing tension in the believer.

> The more I pursue God, drawing from his goodness because I am reconciled to him, the more his life flows through me.

Christ's righteousness in me is fixed, and I am accepted before God. My declared justification before God is permanent. He has reconciled me to himself, and nothing can alter my established position. But my habits of thought, my affections, and my behaviors are accustomed to sin. I need to be refocused and re-trained in the goodness of God by the grace of God, according to the newness of God that he planted in me. My transformation is not just an idealized objective, but a very attainable prospect and expectation for me because I am *in Christ*. The spiritual giant – the apostle Paul, served Christ with abandon yet called himself the "foremost" of sinners having been "a blasphemer, persecutor, and insolent opponent" (1 Timothy 1:15,13).

The more I pursue God, drawing from his goodness because I am reconciled to him, the more his life flows through me. Just like the life of the tree flows through the branch because it is vitally connected – the branch is *abiding* in it. As God's Spirit is transforming me at the level of my affections and attitudes, the more I will want to do the things that are aligned with his character and purpose. The more I think his thoughts, love what he loves, and walk in his steps, the more I will recognize the things that are opposed to his perfect goodness as self-destructive. The more I walk with Christ, the more I become like him.

> Our greatest command is to love God; it follows that our highest function is to love God.

Behavior begins in the heart (affections) and the mind (attitudes). We pursue what we desire. It may be helpful to understand sin as misdirected love. Our greatest command is to love God;

it follows that our highest function is to love God. That is why God is transforming us from the inside out. This process of life-change is possible because of Christ and expected for those who are in Christ.

> You must no longer walk as the Gentiles (*unbelieving peoples*) do, in the futility of their minds. They are darkened in their understanding, alienated from the life of God because of the ignorance that is in them, due to their hardness of heart. They have become callous and have given themselves up to sensuality, greedy to practice every kind of impurity. But that is not the way you learned Christ! — assuming that you have heard about him and were taught in him, as the truth is in Jesus, to put off your old self, which belongs to your former manner of life and is corrupt through deceitful desires, and to be renewed in the spirit of your minds, and to put on the new self, created after the likeness of God in true righteousness and holiness (Ephesians 4:17–24 emphasis added).

Doing things *for* God is not the same as walking with God.

The phrase "walking with God" can be misunderstood as doing all the things that a *good* Christian is supposed to do. Doing things *for* God is not the same as walking *with* God. At the time of this writing, a major news headline is the exposure of numerous pastors accused of sexual abuse and the exposure of a network of coverup in order to avoid a bad reputation. This is a perfect example of a branch that is grafted into the tree but is withering – functioning as though it were still cut off from the tree. The real possibility exists that a person united with Christ may be starving himself spiritually (1 Corinthians 3:1-3), resulting in unregenerate behavior that dishonors Christ. Paul confronted the Corinthian believers that this behavior was incongruous with their union with Christ. To *walk with God*, rather, means to relationally pursue the one who made me, loves me, and reconciled me. I draw life from him, which grows this new nature, replacing the passionate demands of the flesh habituated in sin.

> Righteousness is not just a stamp on my life. It is a reality at the core of my being that manifests itself as I am transformed by God's grace.

My regeneration in Christ makes possible the righteousness of Christ moving outward so it is not just an inward reality, but it becomes an outward reality in my behaviors. Righteousness is not just a stamp on my life. It is a reality at the core of my being that manifests itself as I am transformed by God's grace. Paul affirmed this beautifully:

God has done what the law, weakened by the flesh, could not do. By sending his own Son in the likeness of sinful flesh and for sin, he condemned sin in the flesh, in order that the righteous requirement of the law might be fulfilled in us, who walk not according to the flesh but according to the Spirit. For those who live according to the flesh set their minds on the things of the flesh, but those who live according to the Spirit set their minds on the things of the Spirit. For to set the mind on the flesh is death, but to set the mind on the Spirit is life and peace. For the mind that is set on the flesh is hostile to God, for it does not submit to God's law; indeed, it cannot. Those who are in the flesh cannot please God. You, however, are not in the flesh but in the Spirit, if in fact the Spirit of God dwells in you. Anyone who does not have the Spirit of Christ does not belong to him (Romans 8:3-9).

The text above focuses on where I *set my mind*. What informs, shapes, and anchors my affections and my attitudes? Jesus made it clear: these things are the fountainhead of my behavior (Luke 6:45). Hence, the apostle's call to "be transformed by the renewal of your mind" (Romans 12:2).

Sadly, I am convinced that much of the church has forgotten, neglected, or misunderstood these profound truths of regeneration in Scripture. Many who claim the name of Christ are ignorant of their identity and resource in Christ. Instead, we invoke the power of the flesh, religious programs, or theological sharpness to produce in us our purpose as Christians. Objective truths of Scripture remain just that: cold, impersonal concepts that do not produce real change in our lives. This is *not* the gospel of grace. John Ortberg illustrates this well:

> Conforming to boundary markers too often substitutes for authentic transformation.
>
> The church I grew up in had its boundary markers. A prideful or resentful pastor could have kept his job, but if ever the pastor was caught smoking a cigarette, he would've been fired. Not because anyone in the church actually thought smoking a worse sin than pride or resentment, but because smoking defined who was in our subculture and who wasn't, it was a boundary marker.
>
> As I was growing up, having a "quiet time" became a boundary marker, a measure of spiritual growth. If someone had asked me about my spiritual life, I would immediately

think, *Have I been having regular and lengthy quiet time?* My initial thought was not, *Am I growing more loving toward God and toward people?*

Boundary markers change from culture to culture, but the dynamic remains the same. If people do not experience authentic transformation, then their faith will deteriorate into a search for the boundary markers that masquerade as evidence of a changed life.[22]

Could it be that I am a dry, thirsty branch even though I may be vitally connected to the tree? The remedy to my dryness is *not* more religious activity or attempting to make my life more *Christian* by pure grit or servile duty. Such activity often resorts to keeping up Christian appearances. This fakery is the same as pinning some fruit to a branch then clamoring to be noticed that my branch has successfully produced fruit. The gospel of grace calls us not to a creed, a philosophy, or a specific lifestyle — but to God.

> The remedy to my dryness is *not* more religious activity or attempting to make my life more *Christian* by pure grit or servile duty.

---

[22] John Ortberg, *"True (and False) Transformation," Leadership* (Summer 2002), p. 102

Habits of Regeneration

To grow and be transformed into the image of Jesus, I must pursue God. To encourage Christians to be labor-intensive in their walk with God, I teach four Scriptural activities that I call the *habits of regeneration.*

- **Draw near to God.** "Draw near to God, and he will draw near to you" (James 4:8). Walk and interact with your Creator/Redeemer now that you are reconciled to him.

- **Abide in Christ.** "Abide in me, and I in you. As the branch cannot bear fruit by itself, unless it abides in the vine, neither can you, unless you abide in me. I am the vine; you are the branches. Whoever abides in me and I in him, he it is that bears much fruit, for apart from me you can do nothing" (John 15:4-5). Draw life from Jesus Christ as you find yourself at home in his presence.

- **Walk by the Spirit.** "Walk by the Spirit, and you will not gratify the desires of the flesh" (Galatians 5:16). Through your communion with God grow in your sensitivity to his inner witness, his trans-forming power, and illumination of God's word.

> Draw life from Jesus Christ as you find yourself at home in his presence.

- **Let the word of Christ dwell in you richly.** "Let the word of Christ dwell in you richly, teaching and admonishing one another in all wisdom, singing psalms and hymns and spiritual songs, with thankfulness in your hearts to God" (Colossians 3:16). Let God's Word, his self-disclosure, inform and transform your attitudes and affections.

> Let God's Word, his self-disclosure, inform and transform your attitudes and affections.

The unregenerate person cannot practice these four habits of regeneration. According to our new nature and the power of the Holy Spirit, we can. When we pursue God by practicing these habits we develop and experience what God desires for us. The branch that is drawing life from the tree does not need to exert effort to produce fruit. The fruit, rather, is the *natural outflow* of the branch drawing life from the tree. It must be noted that this does not eliminate obedience from the believer's life. But our attitudes and desires are what drive our actions. Mere external conformity to moral behavior is not the gospel of grace. God's grace, rather,

> The branch that is drawing life from the tree does not need to exert effort to produce fruit. The fruit, rather, is the natural outflow of the branch drawing life from the tree.

creates a revolution in me that moves me from darkness to light, from death to life, from brokenness to newness. By his grace I am changed, and I am a part of the change that God desires in my world. I need to hear my Creator and Redeemer saying to me through his Word, his self-disclosure, and the inner witness of his Spirit, "I have reconciled you to myself. I am your life, your satisfaction, and your reward. Come, draw near, and abide in me. Then live in the outflow of my righteousness."

> And you, who once were alienated and hostile in mind, doing evil deeds, he has now reconciled in his body of flesh by his death, in order to present you holy and blameless and above reproach before him. (Colossians 1:21–22)

Think About It

1. What is the difference between conformity and transformation?

2. How does regeneration upend the notion "That's just the way I am"?

3. How do transformed desires and thoughts lead to obedience?

4. What steps will you take to develop the habits of regeneration?

Conclusion

John Lennon's widow, Yoko Ono, once called for the anniversary of her husband's death to become a day of worldwide healing. In 2006, she placed a full-page ad in the *New York Times* with the following pledge: "Let's wish strongly that one day we will be able to say that we healed ourselves, and by healing ourselves, we healed the world."[23] Her plea seems consistent with one of Lennon's most memorable songs.

> Imagine there's no heaven, it's easy if you try;
> no hell below us, above us, only sky.
> Imagine all the people livin' for today, Ah!
> Imagine there's no countries, it isn't hard to do;
> nothing to kill or die for, and no religion, too…[24]

Lennon's song is an example of a branch imagining that it can thrive away from the tree from which it pulls its life. This has not worked. It cannot work. Not only

---

[23] *"Good Week for...All Humanity," The Week (12-8-06), p.4*

[24] Lyrics.com, STANDS4 LLC, 2022. *"Imagine Lyrics."* Accessed July 16, 2022. https://www.lyrics.com/lyric/3403160/John+Lennon/Imagine.

can we not heal ourselves, but also left to ourselves we are hopeless. How many wars in the last century have been fought out of ambition for a theorized utopia?

I have cut many branches from trees in my yard. Initially, they look like they are still alive with hardy green leaves, but their perceived life is fleeting. Eventually they wither and die. Such is the condition of humanity. Any attempt at life severed from the tree is fleeting and delusional. Just as a severed branch must return to the tree, the basic need of humanity is to be reconciled to the one who is the creator and sustainer of life. The good news is that God is loving and good. In his grace, he established the foundation of righteousness for our reconciliation to him.

Not only can we not heal ourselves, but also left to ourselves we are hopeless.

Reformer, Martin Luther, composed the hymn "A Mighty Fortress is Our God" five hundred years ago. The second verse of the hymn paints a succinct picture of our inadequacy and God's gracious provision through Jesus Christ:

Did we in our own strength confide,
our striving would be losing,
were not the right Man on our side,
the Man of God's own choosing.
You ask who that may be? Christ Jesus, it is he;

Lord Sabaoth[25] his name, from age to
age the same;
and he must win the battle.[26]

I played basketball in high school with the dubious distinction of being first man off the bench. One day in practice, Coach scrimmaged the "A" team against the "B" team – an assortment of less talented players. I was on the "B" team. You might think that sounds unfair and that winning for the "B" team was an utterly hopeless endeavor. Normally, that would have been true were it not for one key factor: Coach played for the "B" team. Despite this obvious advantage, for the first few minutes of the scrimmage, we failed miserably. All of us were so self-focused on proving ourselves as worthy that we ignored our coach. After a while of scrimmage, Coach called a time out and drew us into a huddle. I have never forgotten his words: "I am your star player. Get the ball to me." From that moment, there was a fundamental change in our game strategy, and we gave the "A" team a beating. We could never have improved ourselves

> But when this man, who would have been the poster boy for ambition and good works, encountered Christ, he experienced radical change.

---

[25] Lord of Hosts

[26] www.hymnary.org/text/a_mighty_fortress_is_our_god_a_bulwark, Accessed 8/15/2022

enough to win against them; but with the right man on our side, victory was sweet.

Paul had a similar experience as a religious man. He was very focused on laying it all out there to prove himself worthy. But when this man, who would have been the poster boy for ambition and good works, encountered Christ, he experienced radical change.

> Whatever gain I had, I counted as loss for the sake of Christ. Indeed, I count everything as loss because of the surpassing worth of knowing Christ Jesus my Lord. For his sake I have suffered the loss of all things and count them as rubbish, in order that I may gain Christ (Philippians 3:7-8).

From that encounter on, Paul championed "the righteousness from God that depends on faith" (v.9) with one ambition: "that I may know him." The more you know God, the more you will delight in him. The more you delight in him, the more you will love him. The more you love him, the more you will be satisfied in him. The more you are satisfied in him, the more you will point people to him. That is how the gospel of grace works, and there is no greater certification than the gospel lived.

> How precious is your steadfast love, O God! The children of mankind take refuge

in the shadow of your wings. They feast on the abundance of your house, and you give them drink from the river of your delights. For with you is the fountain of life; in your light do we see light (Psalm 36:7-9).

Recommended Reading

Christ Crucified: Understanding the Atonement by Donald Macleod. This book traces how the death of Christ so long ago paid for the sin of humanity today.

Birthright: Christian, Do You Know Who You Are? by David Needham. The author explains the realities and implications of regeneration, and the believer's new nature and identity in Christ.

All Things New: The Significance of Newness for Biblical Theology by Carl B. Hock, Jr. This author presents a thorough treatment on the subject of newness.

In My Place Condemned He Stood: Celebrating the Glory of the Atonement by J.I. Packer and Mark Dever. The authors give a clear presentation of the doctrine of Christ's death for our sins and that through his death he paid the price for our sins by penal substitution.

The Finished work of Christ by Francis Schaeffer. This work is an insightful treatment of the first eight chapters of Romans focusing on justification through faith in Christ.

The Gospel of Jesus Christ by Paul Washer. A rendering of the gospel including God's character, man's sin problem and Christ's redemption.

Acknowledgments

The Xulon Publishing team and Salem Author Services faithfully guided me through the process of getting this material printed and into the hands of many.

Deep appreciation for my administrative assistant, Ella Billman. You've been with this project from the beginning, and you have been a great encouragement along the way.

Thank you Aprille Donaldson for your passion for this material and your invaluable help in crafting the document at its early stages.

Unspeakable gratitude to Darrel and Mary Jane Johnson for your tenacious and gracious encouragement for this book. Your love for solid biblical communication is inspiring.

I have so much love and gratitude for the people of Grace Bible Church in Winston-Salem, NC for your support and encouragement, and your desire for clear and faithful exposition of the Scriptures. Your joy of living *in* God's grace is my joy.

To my wife, Andrea – thank you! I love you. Your partnership in life and work has been an encouraging aid and a solid pillar in the joys and challenges through it all.

Finally, I must thank my dad, Harry D. Powell, Jr. (1928-1994) for demonstrating a deep love for God's Word. It has stuck with me.

Thanks be to God.

CPSIA information can be obtained
at www.ICGtesting.com
Printed in the USA
LVHW080800151222
735276LV00004B/179

9 781662 866920